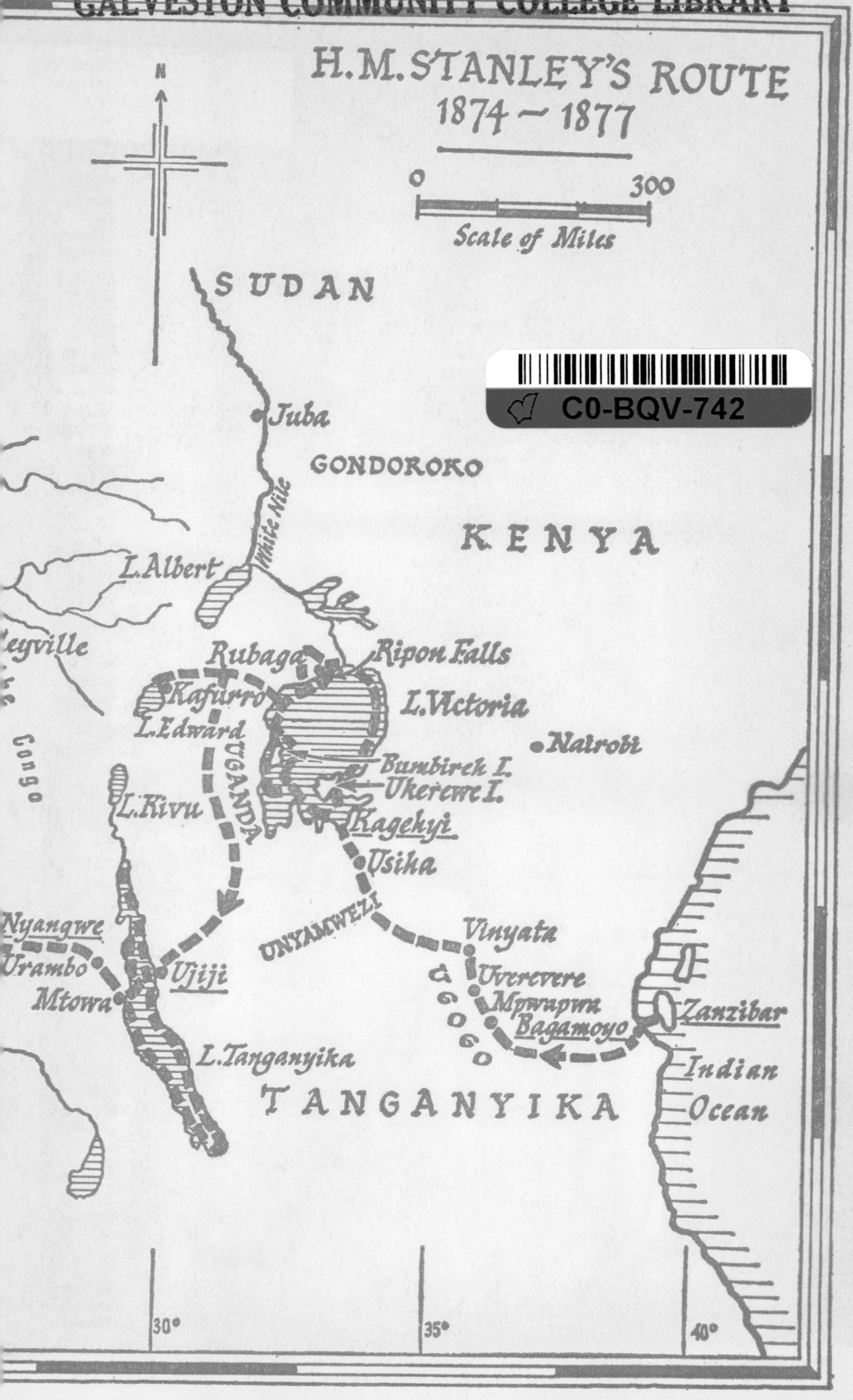
H.M. STANLEY'S ROUTE
1874 — 1877
N
0
300
Scale of Miles
SUDAN
Juba
GONDOROKO
White Nile
KENYA
L.Albert
eyville
Rubaga
Ripon Falls
Kafurro
L.Victoria
L.Edward
Nairobi
Congo
UGANDA
Bumbireh I.
Ukerewe I.
L.Kivu
Kagehyi
Usiha
UNYAMWEZI
Vinyata
Nyangwe
Urambo
Ujiji
Uverevere
Mtowa
UGOGO
Mpwapwa
Zanzibar
Bagamoyo
Indian
Ocean
L.Tanganyika
TANGANYIKA
30°
35°
40°

THE EXPLORATION DIARIES
OF
H. M. STANLEY

THE
EXPLORATION DIARIES
OF
H. M. STANLEY

**Now first published from the
original manuscripts**

EDITED BY

RICHARD STANLEY

AND

ALAN NEAME

NEW YORK
THE VANGUARD PRESS, INC.

CONTENTS

INTRODUCTION

The Discovery of the Manuscripts
Page vii

The Explorer
Page viii

The Second Central African Expedition
Page x

The Places and People
Page xii

The Manuscripts
Page xiv

The Edition
Page xviii

PART ONE

NOVEMBER 12TH, 1874 – FEBRUARY 28TH, 1875

ZANZIBAR – LAKE VICTORIA
Page 23

PART TWO

MARCH 1ST, 1875 – MAY 8TH, 1875

CIRCUMNAVIGATION OF LAKE VICTORIA
Page 61

Contents

PART THREE

MAY 9TH, 1875 – JULY 31ST, 1876

LAKE VICTORIA – LAKE TANGANYIKA
Page 79

PART FOUR

AUGUST, 1876 – AUGUST, 1877

LAKE TANGANYIKA – THE ATLANTIC OCEAN
Page 127

vi

INTRODUCTION

THE DISCOVERY OF THE MANUSCRIPTS

When H. M. Stanley died in 1904 his fame reposed four-square on spectacular achievements set out in his principal published works. Some unpublished material remained in the guarded care of his family, in particular a diary relating to the explorer's pursuit and identification of the River Congo.

When examination revealed the diary to be an incomplete record covering no more than the first nine months of a thousand-day expedition, and when further search failed to reveal any other diaries, the missing original documents of the Congo Expedition were presumed irretrievably lost, destroyed by the explorer himself perhaps, mislaid beyond recall or swept away amongst the bomb damage during the war.

It was only, and highly appropriately, at the time of the Congo Independence celebrations to which the explorer's grandson was invited as official representative of 'Bula Matari, Breaker of Rocks'—as his grandfather, the creator of the original Free State, was known—that Richard Stanley lighted on four closely-written reporter's pads in a box-file, among other box-files of neatly labelled bills, receipts, and so forth in the explorer's hand, at Furzehill Place, Pirbright, his country seat and last home.

These undistinguished-looking pads proved to be manuscripts of the deepest interest. They were the *tara-tara*, the fetish-papers so rightly dreaded by the Chiefs of Mowa in May, 1877, the contents of which were to revolutionise the lives of millions in the Congo and in Belgium. The pads were the day-to-day account of an astounding journey, entered in forest camp or collapsible boat, fair or foul weather, poorly fed or downright starving, by the explorer in days before the course of the River Congo was more than a myth or its known waters charted fifty miles beyond the Atlantic coast of Africa.

These little books held the raw record of a resolution, an effort, an achievement in the order of Xenophon's march from

Babylon to the Bosphorus—only Xenophon had his thousands, and Stanley but a handful; abrupt, matter-of-fact, repetitive, encyclopaedic, tense, enthralling transcripts of a fervid will to conquer and achieve.

The documents will be more fully described later in this Introduction. Here only be it said that through them we ourselves make a discovery: of the intrepid, unswerving man behind the expansive brilliance of a successful explorer-author. The robes in which a hero-worshipping century invested him, the armour in which his own high-mindedness and journalistic talent insulated him, have not yet been put on. We see Stanley without posture, without concession, without consideration of any other reader than himself or, in the darkest moments, his executors; alone among illiterates and enemies, often too weary to enthuse, too feverish to write, sometimes too miserable to spell, and always too determined to admit defeat or die.

THE EXPLORER

Sir Henry Morton Stanley, G.C.B., the hero who found Livingstone, and first circumnavigated Lakes Victoria and Tanganyika, who first travelled the length of the River Congo, who laid the foundations of the Congo Free State and rescued Emin Pasha from the armies of the Mahdi, was not born great. His interior conquest of the first eighteen miserable years of his life, no less than his exterior conquest of Central African geography, affirms and vindicates the power of human will to triumph over circumstance. If Stanley's formal writings display all the sententiousness of the nineteenth century, it was perhaps only in the moral climate of the Victorian Age that such a crippling challenge could meet with so magnificent a response.

The most comprehensive account of the career from humble origin to distinguished conclusion is to be found in his own published works. All subsequent biographers, while correcting emphasis or clarifying detail, have drawn so extensively on Stanley's own writings that there is no need to retrace a familiar life-history beyond the salient events.

Stanley was not born of great family. Indeed, he was not even born Stanley. The son of obscure and unwed parents, he first saw light in Denbigh, Wales, in 1841 and was baptised in the name of John Rowlands. At the age of six he was consigned to St. Asaph Union Workhouse, where he remained until he ran away at the age of fifteen. In 1859 he arrived penniless in New Orleans, having shipped across the Atlantic as a cabin-boy. An American broker called Stanley employed him, adopted him and rebaptised him in the name which was to resound across the world.

At the age of twenty Stanley played a very minor part in the American Civil War. In 1867, as a newspaper reporter, he accompanied General Hancock's expedition against the Red Indians. In 1869, travelling in the Near East as a reporter for the *New York Herald*, he earned a name for himself by scooping the defeat and suicide of King Theodore of Abyssinia.

In 1871, commissioned by the *New York Herald*, Stanley set out from Zanzibar on his first Central African Expedition, to discover the whereabouts of David Livingstone who had been rumoured dead. Stanley found the ageing missionary-explorer at Ujiji on the shores of Lake Tanganyika, spent four 'indescribably happy' months in his company and returned from Africa in 1872 to fame, controversy and a round of lectures in England and the United States.

In 1874, with the joint backing of the *Daily Telegraph* and the *New York Herald*, Stanley launched his second Central African Expedition, of which the diaries in this book are a daily record. The Expedition crossed Africa from Zanzibar on the East Coast to Boma on the West and ended in 1877. His full-length account of this Expedition, entitled *Through the Dark Continent*, consisting of two octavo volumes with many maps and engravings, appeared in 1879.

Two years after the Expedition, Stanley returned to the vast territory he had traversed, this time with the task of organising it, on behalf of Leopold II, King of the Belgians, and the International African Association, into what in 1885 became known as the Congo Free State.

In 1887 Stanley conducted his third Central African Expedition, the aim of which was to relieve Emin Pasha, the beleaguered Governor of Sudanese Equatoria. This time he crossed Africa in the reverse direction, from the mouth of the River Congo to Zanzibar. In his third, as in his two previous Expeditions, Stanley accomplished his mission.

Whereas his first two Expeditions had been in the one case philanthropic and in the second scientific, the third was a Mission of State and Stanley returned from it a national hero.

He married Dorothy Tennant in Westminster Abbey in 1890; subsequently he explored no more. He was elected Member of Parliament for North Lambeth (Liberal Unionist), received a Knighthood, and retired full of honours to Furzehill Place near Pirbright in 1900. Having no children, he and his wife adopted a son. Four years later he died, aged sixty-four, and was buried in the village churchyard.

THE SECOND CENTRAL AFRICAN EXPEDITION, 1874–1877.

The terms of reference for the 1874 Expedition as announced by its sponsors were extraordinarily wide: "The purpose of the enterprise is to complete the work left unfinished by the lamented death of Doctor Livingstone; to solve, if possible, the remaining problems of the geography of Central Africa; and to investigate and report upon the haunts of the slave-traders."

These tasks, as resolved by Stanley, became more precisely: the thorough investigation of Lake Victoria; the thorough investigation of Lake Tanganyika; and the exploration of the western part of Central Africa which in 1874 was still a blank on the maps.

At that time, Central African studies were still largely orientated towards the discovery of the sources of the Nile. John Hanning Speke, exploring Lake Victoria in 1862, had discovered the Ripon Falls by which the Nile emerges from the northern shore of that vast lake. But his solution to the age-long mystery was not readily approved by contemporary authorities on African geography; Richard Burton, inspired by mixed motives, never accepted Speke's identification of them as long as he lived. David Livingstone also rejected Speke's discovery, persisting in his own notion that the great River Lualaba, flowing northward through Nyangwe as though to the distant Mediterranean, was the head water of the Nile. Meanwhile, none of the explorers who had reached Lake Victoria had either sailed right round it or found out whether this huge expanse of water was one colossal lake or even as many as five contiguous ones.

Of the nature of Lake Tanganyika similar doubts were entertained. No one was sure whether it was one lake or two, or whether any river flowed out of it which might conceivably serve Lake Victoria or the Nile.

Finally, with regard to the western part of Central Africa, nothing whatever was known at first hand of the territories between Nyangwe and the Atlantic coastal strip more than a thousand miles to westward.

One of the principal features of this Atlantic coast was the immense estuary of the River Congo in South Latitude 6°, but the Congo Expedition of 1816, under Captain Tuckey, had made little headway in their exploration of the river on account of frightful cataracts, the farthest up-country of which they dubbed 'Tuckey's Farthest' and plotted in the wrong position on their maps.

The mouth of the River Congo was two degrees of latitude south of Nyangwe, so distant from the coast. It was therefore audacious of Lieutenant Cameron, R.N. (1874), to suggest that the River Lualaba and the River Congo might be identical, especially since at Nyangwe the River Lualaba flowed northward (though significantly with a bias to the west) as far as native tongue could report.

Stanley's Expedition was intended to settle these three questions. And the haunts of the slave-traders could conveniently be investigated on the way, for the staging-posts for the Expedition at Ujiji on Lake Tanganyika and at Nyangwe on the River Lualaba were both Arab trading depots where the traders dealt chiefly in slaves.

It was not therefore a primary purpose of the Expedition to cross Central Africa from coast to coast. This feat had been performed already by Livingstone (1854–1856), though where the continent was very much narrower to the south, and Cameron repeated it before Stanley's Expedition had been more than eighteen months on the march. The main object of Stanley's Expedition, as he put on record in the second entry in his day-book (November 17th, 1874) was 'The Discovery of the Nile and Congo Sources'. If the Rivers Lualaba and Congo proved identical however, the crossing of

xi

the continent would be a necessary condition for demonstrating their identity. As late as November 9th, 1876, as will be seen from the entry in the day-book, Stanley still had not made up his mind whether to strike for the Atlantic coast or to return by a north-easterly route to Gondoroko (Gondokoro) on the White Nile, discharge his men there and himself go home via Cairo. The Expedition was equipped on a scale that made either decision feasible.

Setting out from Zanzibar on November 12th, 1874, the Expedition reached Boma on August 9th, 1877.

THE PLACES AND PEOPLE

In the undiscovered Africa of the last century, an explorer could still exercise the two functions proper to his craft. He could explore with a view to proving or disproving a theory—in Stanley's case that the Rivers Lualaba and Congo were one; and he could still have the excitement of discovering and satisfaction of describing places and peoples that had never been seen by European eyes before.

Hence, Stanley's daily record of the Expedition's progress is peppered with outlandish place-names. Of many of those mentioned, little can really be said by way of illumination except that the Expedition passed through them, or heard of them. As Stanley varied his spelling of these names the more familiar he grew with the language of each locality, we have regularised them to accord with his published account of the journey in *Through the Dark Continent.*

Entries in the day-books are normally headed with the name of the place which the Expedition had reached at the end of any given day; sometimes this place-name is followed by the name of the tribal region—for as yet there were no colonial frontiers in Central Africa.

As Stanley traced the course of the River Lualaba onwards from Nyangwe, which he left on November 5th, 1876, he found that the river was known by different names in successive tribal areas. He re-named it in honour of Livingstone, mindful that in following this unexplored waterway he was in a literal sense completing the labours of his master and friend. It was not until February 7th, 1877, that he received certain confirmation that the Livingstone River and the River Congo were one single stream. Twenty-two years after this identity had been established, the upper reaches of the River Congo still figured as the Livingstone River on a map in the second edition of *Through the Dark Continent*.

As regards the swarms of human beings mentioned by name, it is helpful at once to distinguish the discoverers from the discovered.

The European section of the Expedition consisted of Stanley himself, thirty-three years of age at the outset though white-haired by the conclusion; Frederick Barker, formerly a clerk in a London hotel, who acted as accountant to the Expedition until his death at Kagehyi in April, 1875; and the brothers Edward and Francis Pocock, sons of a Kentish fisherman. Edward Pocock was bugler to the Expedition until he died of typhus at Chiwyu (Suna) in January, 1875. Francis, nearly always referred to in the day-books as Frank, acted as Stanley's deputy whenever the explorer was absent from the main body of his men, and as adjutant when he was present, until he was drowned in the River Congo in June, 1877.

The rank and file of the Expedition, recruited from the mixed inhabitants of the Zanzibar Coast, are collectively referred to as the Wangwana. A number of these had attended Stanley on his search for Livingstone in 1871. Of these:

Manwa Sera was appointed Chief Captain of the Expedition, and Chowpereh, Wadi Rehani, Kacheche, Farjalla, Zaidi, Wadi Safeni, Mabruki, Ferahan, who all make appearances in the following pages, were appointed chiefs among the two hundred and thirty men who signed on at Zanzibar; Uledi was the coxswain of Stanley's boat *The Lady Alice*; Billali was his gun-bearer; and Kalulu, whom he had taken to England and America in 1872, was his personal page.

Associated with the Expedition from Nyangwe to Vinya-Njara was the Arab magnate, adventurer and slave-master Tippu-Tib. His subordinates, Muini Dugumbi and Mtago-moyo, were slavers almost as notorious as himself. Tippu-Tib's four hundred strong-men who acted as escort to the Expedition through the rain forest from November 5th to December 28th, 1876, are collectively referred to as the Wanyamwezi. Tippu-Tib had been helpful to Cameron and was later to play an equivocal part in Stanley's third Expedition, the relief of Emin Pasha.

Among the discovered were notably: Mtesa, King of Uganda, with the officials of his court and his senior officers, Admiral Magassa and General Sambuzi; Rumanika, King of Karagwe; and Mirambo, Lord of a confederation of bandits known as the Ruga-Ruga. Of these potentates, both Mtesa and Rumanika had already been visited by other explorers, and Mirambo was well-known by the terror of his name.

To these add a host of tribal chiefs, sometimes known by their personal name, sometimes by the name of their principal seat; and the tribal multitudes themselves. The prefix *U-* indicates country, *Wa-* the people who dwell in it: thus, the Waganda are the inhabitants of Uganda. One man of Uganda is a *M*ganda. The language he speaks is *Ki*-ganda. Apart from these Swahili prefixes, Stanley does not use many native words: *tembe* means a house; *boma*, a stockade or stockaded village; *manioc* and *cassava* are two names for the tapioca plant; *banghi* is the wild hemp, a narcotic; *doti* is a measure of cloth; *honga* is transit tribute; and *pagazi*, a native porter and guide. Sometimes the day-books make little distinction between territory and inhabitants: the Manyema, for instance, are the ruthless inhabitants of Manyema (Manyuema), a tribal area to the west of Lake Tanganyika.

THE MANUSCRIPTS

The hitherto unedited daily records of the 1874 Expedition consist of:

  i. a Charles Letts folio-size Perpetual Diary, and
  ii. four good quality reporter's note-pads.

The Perpetual Diary contains the day-to-day record of progress of the Expedition from the Island of Zanzibar (November, 1874) to Kagehyi on the shore of Lake Victoria (February, 1875); Stanley's circumnavigation of Lake Victoria and first visit to the King of Uganda (March–April, 1875); and the voyage of the entire Expedition from Kagehyi across the lake to Dumo in the territories of this friendly King (May–August, 1875). Stanley has drawn a line under the daily entries and in the remaining space, without regard to date, has written a continuous narrative of King Mtesa's campaign against the Wavuma (August–October, 1875) and the part the author himself played in it. A short History of Uganda, essays on Life and Manners in Uganda and a set of accounts fill the blank pages at the beginning and end of the book.

The daily entries are illustrated by elegant sketch-maps of the Expedition's route and of contiguous sections of the coast of Lake Victoria; and by sketches of King Mtesa's court, the floating fortress that Stanley designed for the confounding of the rebels; fish, weapons, anatomies and local dignitaries.

The condition of the Perpetual Diary, the fact that all the entries are in ink, very neatly and consistently written, and that edited material from the first reporter's note-pad is contained in it, indicate that this is a fair-copy book compiled between May 10th and the middle of October, 1875, during periods of leisure at Kagehyi and at the battle headquarters of the King of Uganda.

If the Perpetual Diary is fascinating to study, the note-pads are even more so. They cover the periods:

   i. August 15th, 1875 to February 29th, 1876;

  ii. March 2nd, 1876 to July 30th, 1876;

 iii. August 21st, 1876 to March 3rd, 1877;

 iv. March 4th, 1877, to August 10th, 1877;

and contain Stanley's raw impressions before he trimmed, expanded or recast them.

Comparison of these note-pads with those passages quoted in *Through the Dark Continent* as being direct transcripts from 'my diary' shows a wide divergence between the two texts. For example, one of the most dramatic moments in the story of the Expedition occurred on February 7th, 1877, when Stanley for the first time heard the name Congo applied by a native tongue to the Livingstone (Lualaba) River. In the third note-pad, the entry for this date, as will be seen, deals mainly with the problem of food supplies but bears a marginal jotting without comment: 'River called Ikuta Yacongo'. In the corresponding 'diary extract' of *Through the Dark Continent*, these four pregnant words have farrowed into a set-piece for a chapter-ending:

Before leaving the Chief of Rubunga's presence, I asked him the name of the river, in a mongrel mixture of Ki-swahili, Kinyamwezi, Kijiji, Ki-regga, and Ki-Kusu. He understood after a while, and replied it was 'Ibari'. But after he had quite comprehended the drift of the question, he replied in a sonorous voice: '*Ikutu ya Kongo!*'

There had really been no doubt in my mind since we had left the Stanley Falls that the terrible river would prove eventually to be the river of Congo-land, but it was very agreeable to be told so . . .

From this and from other comparisons it can be seen that the so-called 'extracts from my diary' in *Through the Dark Continent* are hardly more than a device for varying the type-face, for they are quite as deliberately composed as the rest of the narrative.

It is also instructive of Stanley's talents as a writer and self-editor to compare the long, passionate, even reproachful, lamentation at the death of Frank Pocock in the note-pad entry of June 3rd, 1877, with the noble and restrained last tribute paid to his companion in the corresponding pages of *Through the Dark Continent* (ii. 314–315).

The note-pads, despite their vicissitudes through jungles and down cataracts, are in excellent condition. Their paper is a little yellowed from age, but never stained by tea or coffee, nor is there one single tropical insect squashed between their many pages—an indication of the care with which Stanley treated them. Almost all the entries are in pencil, though occasionally during a protracted halt Stanley inked some of them over later. Such was his care at this exercise that where original entries were pencilled with a fever-shaken hand, Stanley faithfully followed the contours of the palsied script with his pen. The entries on the whole are wonderfully legible, the notable exception being the account of the death of Frank Pocock when Stanley was labouring under strong emotion. The pages abound in sketch-maps, drawings of native dress, landscapes, waterfalls, villages, remarkable fish, utensils and weapons; Stanley was strong on mapping, still-life and land-scape. His sketches of human anatomy are less convincing.

The spare pages of these pads, unlike those of the Perpetual

Diary with its draft chapters for *Through the Dark Continent,* are covered in calculations of latitude and longitude, lists of personnel, inveterate idlers, wages, loads, camps, possible chapter headings, glossaries, thefts, &c., while the miscellanea of the third pad include the draft of a lugubrious poem:

> Must I still continue the quest
>   Of this strange & wandering stream
> A prey to this gloomy land's pest
>   And banished from sunlight or gleam
>
> The natives declare it flows North
>   The Savants describe its course West
> Livingstone all his powers put forth
>   To win the strange secret, and rest
>
> Livingstone was old but loyal
>   Of a courageous heart and well tried
> He roused up his soul for the trial
>   He made a supreme effort & died
>
> Then Cameron came to the field
>   Young, stout-hearted, eager & brave
> But the river refused to yield
>   The knowledge of the flow of its wave
>
> Westward from Tanganyika's shore
>   We flew to the trial of might
> Determined to die or explore
>   The wild lands which stood on its right
>
> At Nyangwe where they both turned away
>   We learned what dangers opposed
> And to avoid what led them astray
>   On ourselves we firmly reposed
>
> Through Uregga's cheerless gloom
>   And its forests so lone and drear
> As under a sense of impending doom
>   We travelled ten days . . .
>
> Our people lamented aloud . . .

Happily Stanley's mood changed; he left the poem unfinished and unpunctuated; the low-spirited verses are acutely unmusical. But most remarkably, in two and a half years of hardship, he only twice committed his low spirits to his note-pads—in the rain forest of Uregga (November 1876), where this poem was composed, and in the days following Frank Pocock's death (June 1877). Otherwise, when disasters occurred, when the trusted failed, he recorded a motion of impatience and rejection, turning his attention forthwith to the future. For instance, see the entry for January 4th, 1875.

He wrote very little of his feelings, much about his actions, orders, decisions. It is a tireless resilience more than any other personal quality that the reporter's pads convey.

ALAN NEAME

THE EDITION

In preparing these manuscripts for publication we have reduced the material by about one sixth. Entries larded with names, though they swell the epic theme with their sonority, and those reporting petty misdemeanours of his men, or occasional days of plain-sailing, we have tended to omit. We have also left out material of a topographical, ethnological or reflective kind where that material was obviously put together after the day's events had been recorded or where it refers to circumstances already some time past. All such material, often *verbatim*, was to find a place in *Through the Dark Continent*.

Stanley was a vivid descriptive writer, his powers of observation were most acute, even though his literary style is often complex and over-elaborate to modern taste. The journal of the Expedition would lose much of its immediacy and depth if all descriptive passages were omitted. We have therefore tried as far as possible to include at least one example of the way he treated each of the varied aspects of African life that claimed his sharp and inexhaustible attention.

Where we have felt bound to make excisions, we have done our best to preserve the continuity of Stanley's account. The passages in italics, and they alone, are not from the explorer's hand, but the editors'.

We have divided the material into four parts reflecting Stanley's own resolution of the Expedition's terms of reference. The first part relates the Expedition's course from Zanzibar to Kagehyi on the shore of Lake Victoria; the second comprises the circumnavigation of Lake Victoria and Stanley's adventures as military adviser to the embattled King of Uganda; the third deals with the march from Lake Victoria to Lake Tanganyika and the circumnavigation of the latter; and the last is devoted to the exploration of the River Congo from the Expedition's departure from the shores of Lake Tanganyika to its arrival at Boma, the trading-station on the Atlantic estuary beyond the farthest cataract.

RICHARD STANLEY AND ALAN NEAME

ILLUSTRATIONS

H. M. Stanley after the 1874 expedition . *facing page* 96

Edward and Frank Pocock and the *Lady Alice* . . 97

Camp at Mpwapwa, based on a drawing by the author 112

Mtesa's palace at Rubaga, from a drawing by the author 112

The Ripon Falls, a sketch from the author's notebook . 113

Mtesa I, the Kabaka of Uganda, from a photograph by the author 113

H. M. Stanley with Kalulu. A photograph taken before the expedition left 160

A page from the author's field notebook . . 161

Sketch of Bridge Island, from the author's notebook . 161

The village of Manyema, from a sketch by the Author 176

Battle on the Lualaba 176

Zanzibar, a photograph by the author . . . 177

Journey's end — the arrival at Kabinda . . . 177

PART I

ZANZIBAR—LAKE VICTORIA

November 12th, 1874—February 28th, 1875

ZANZIBAR—LAKE VICTORIA

November 12th, 1874:

Left Zanzibar for Bagamoyo.

End of Ramadan. Today my people were embarked in dhows and sailed for Bagamoyo. 224 answered to their names. I had besides 6 asses and 5 dogs. Our property consisted of 72 bales of cloth, 36 bags of beads, 4 manloads of wire, 14 boxes of assorted stores, 23 boxes of ammunition, 2 loads of photographic materials, 3 loads Europeans' personal baggage, 12 loads of boat, 6 loads pontoons, 1 box medicines, 1 load of cooking utensils and 12 other miscellaneous loads.

November 17th:

The Anglo-American Expedition for the Discovery of the Nile and Congo Sources marched from Bagamoyo for the interior today. Glad was I to quit the trouble and annoyances that beset a traveller at this initial point. Intemperance, Arab malice and such vexations soon demoralise the best organized Expedition if it halts much time at Bagamoyo. Mansur bin Sulieman played the Wali or Governor like another Sancho Panza. Since his return from Mecca with the fanatic Prince of Zanzibar, he has become a very Draco. The sun was intensely hot and seemed to burn through our sun helmets. Castor, the noble mastiff (gift of Baroness Burdett-Coutts) died a mile from Kikoka. The noble Wangwana soldiers who had so stoutly declared a year's advance as their due wilted under the intense heat, and appeared more like images of men than the boisterous intemperate fools who astonished Bagamoyo. Our boat *Lady Alice* did admirable service in the ferriage of the Kingani. The entire Expedition crossed the river in her within two hours.

November 18th:

A halt at Kikoka.

Wrote my letters, and settled all bills. Was visited in camp by Arabs who came to claim their female slaves who had run

25

away from the plantations to become wives of the soldiers. Those they identified were returned.

The soldiers were those members of the Expedition recruited for its protection.

November 19th:

A march to Rosako. Distance 12 miles.

November 20th:

Halt at Rosako.

We mean to proceed leisurely at first until the men are broken to harness and hard work. Vaccinated all who had not already suffered from smallpox.

November 21st:

March to Usigwa county of Kanga. West-north-west 3 hours. $7\frac{1}{2}$ miles.

Route through a beautiful country. Park land dipping into lovely vales and rising into gentle ridges. Water abundant, grass plenty, fat rich soil, sandstone the base of it. Hills of Pongwe in view four miles from Rosako.

November 22nd:

March to Sangarambwe, Usagara, a small bush-encircled village consisting of 8 roomy cone huts, vicinity green as an English lawn. Grand view en-route of a fine and luxuriant country of swelling ridges and subsiding dales. Distance 9 miles.

November 23rd:

Reached Pongwe after a march of 11 miles. Course West by North $\frac{1}{2}$ North. Altitude of village at base of mountain 1150 feet. Mountain is probably 1200 feet higher than village. Greater Pongwe about 1700 feet.

Porters are yet new to carrying burdens. Sore shoulders, blistered feet, sickness, lung disease, spitting of blood and other ailments, distinguish their complaints. We dropped two yesterday, one from a swollen leg, the other from general debility. White men behave very well.

November 24th:

Marched to Congorido. 8 miles West by North.

Pongwe Hills in fine view of village. Congorido is populous. Good *boma* [*stockade*] but water brackish. Good water is obtainable to the south-east.

November 26th:

March to Mfuteh, Useguha. North-west by North. 10½ miles.

Route across similar scenes as before, thin forest with patches of plain country dotted with peaks and solitary cones. One is seen north-west from Congorido. The inhabitants are timid and suspicious. They have built the best-looking village we have yet seen and a wide view of rolling country is visible from the gate of the village.

The baobab begins to be seen, out of which the natives make good rope. The borassus, *doum* [*the fruit of which, according to Stanley, has the taste of stale gingerbiscuits*] and date palm flourish in the vicinity. Near Congorido we crossed a longitudinal depression in the land which scarcely produced a single tree save the *doum* palm. The soil had considerable alkali in it and the water was brackish. Lions are reported to be numerous. Two of our goats were lost. Altitude of Mfuteh 1125 feet.

November 27th:

Reached Changariguah after a march of 8½ miles. Altitude 875 feet.

Wami River flows along our course four miles after leaving Mfuteh. Its banks are fringed with fine tall trees, but beyond these extend grassy plains and thin dwarf forests wherein game is abundant. From village we obtain views of the colossal Mount Kidudu and its less sublime peaks of Nguru.

November 28th:

Camp on Wami River. West ½ North. 11 miles.

The mastiff Captain died yesterday after 5 days illness. Country abounds with game. We travelled along banks of Wami River. Various species of palm are numerous. Gum and other trees, dwarf ebony, and stunted copal are the shrubs most frequently met with.

November 29th:

Reached Rubuti. 7½ miles West ½ North. Altitude 1100 feet above sea.

Rubuti is a village on the Lugumbwa, a creek flowing into the Wami from the base of a rocky mountain rising immediately above it. We crossed the Wami three miles from here. Ford was 2½ feet deep. Granite lumps protruding in several places above river. The Wami reminded me very much of the Prah on the Ashantee Coast. It is about 40 yards wide from bank to bank. Banks are steep and rise about 16 feet above river at its present stage. A singular suspension bridge of netted bark and lianes like a caricature of Niagara suspension bridge forms the means of crossing the river for the natives. We here heard of a French merchant encamped not far off who has lately been trading for ivory at Mpwapwa. Mountains of Nguru rise large and vast in our front.

The Expedition advanced 30½ miles, crossed 5 rivers and passed into the district of Nguru.

December 3rd:

Arrived at Simba-Mwenni's village on the Mkundi River. Altitude 1950 feet above sea.

The Mkundi River divides Nguru from Usagara. The country begins to be more open, the grass has a more sere aspect, trees appear autumn-like. Five villages are in this neighbourhood. The Chief Simba-Mwenni very gracious after explanation. Sent sheep, flour, plantains. Despatched a friendly gift in return. The Wa-nguru speak the same dialect as the Waseguha and Wasagara, and affect the same manners, are fond of brass wire, black and white beads.

December 4th:

Makubika. West by South. 16½ miles distance. Altitude above sea 2675 feet.

It was a long and fatiguing march today. We met but little water on the road. Scenes grand and impressive, peaks and knolls rising in all directions, those of Ukamba famous for its elephants. Near Bow's Back [*The Back of the Bow, a mountain*] a small clear lake is found. Kasigulibi to the north of Mpwapwa. This village is in Kaguru. I discovered by this route that the Mukondokwa or Wami River does not rise in Kaguru, but on its southern frontier.

The Expedition advanced a further 17 *miles through romantic scenery.*

December 7th:

Kitangeh. 6½ miles West-north-west. 3485 feet above sea level.

Route continues to be picturesque. Villages dot every summit and knoll. Kitangeh is rich in cattle and goats. Natives say that Wamasai sometimes make raids upon their cattle, that their country is but three days' march north, that Usagara extends northwards to Masai. Natives extremely suspicious, anything uncommon regarded as indicating hostility. The Mtemi or Chief is a rare beggar, and not inept, if refused, to threaten dire consequences.

December 8th:

Halt at Kitangeh. Ever since leaving Rosako near the coast we have had rain nearly every day.

December 9th:

Camp. 9 miles West by South ½ South.

After ascending from Kitangeh a lengthy slope of one of the chain of hills which encircles the basin of grassy Kitangeh by a gradual ascent to 4475 feet, we beheld a plain stretching northward and westward teeming with varied and noble game. Southward the sterility which marks Ugogo and the immediate countries began to be observable, growing more white and naked as we cast our eyes north-westward. Down in the plain surrounded on all sides but the west by miles of dense thorn shrubs, halfway between a rough-faced hill and three rocky knolls, we pitched camp. Near the latter was discovered a pool of excellent and crystal clear water.

In the afternoon after a rest I sallied out to hunt, accompanied by a burly soldier named Msenna—who had distinguished himself at Zanzibar by many a fatal combat with other ruffian natures like his own—and the famous boy Billali than whom none seemed more born for the hunt and chase than he. The elephant rifle though of heavy weight was his especial burden, because it was almost always of fatal accuracy and productive of food and camp applause for the meat it brought to his comrades.

We crossed a sterile plain and plunged amid thin bush and brake towards a mass formed by two hilly chains which met here from the west and north-east. After half an hour's search I discovered a herd of zebra, and after a little stalking shot two fine fat animals. Billali was dispatched to camp four miles off for men to convey the meat, while Msenna and I prepared it. Meanwhile, just as night was advancing, I saw a lion stalking leisurely nose to ground, sniffing suspiciously as I thought, and coming towards me. I whistled to put Msenna on his guard which alarmed the lion, who after a defiant growl bounded off. Presently a herd of lions, eight or ten in number, was seen emerging from the same direction.

I waited until the foremost was well within reach of a bullet, and shot him dead. The others retreated fast at first, afterwards more slowly, and halted. On looking round for my cartridges I discovered that Billali had taken them with him to camp, so that under the circumstances I thought it more prudent to retire and leave the meat to the lions. Two hours after dark I heard the shouts of the men coming for the meat, to whom we were soon united. Together we made a charge upon our game, and succeeded in conveying every morsel safe to camp by 9 p.m.

December 11th:

Tubugwe. West by South ½ South. 14¼ miles.

Leaving our camp we marched across a plain six miles in width, during which we counted 14 skulls, relics of an unfortunate caravan fallen in battle with Masai marauders who generally lie in wait on the slopes of the adjacent mountains for weak caravans, and distressed porters . . .

December 12th:

Arrived at Mpwapwa. West by South ½ South. 12½ miles.

Trap and conglomerates, gneiss, quartzite and granite with basalt were the rocks visible between Kitangeh and Mpwapwa.

December 13th:

Halt at Mpwapwa.

For description of this place, see *How I Found Livingstone.* I have nothing to add except that provisions were extremely scarce, and at famine prices. Even the natives journeyed far to purchase food for goats and cattle.

December 14th:

Arrived at Chunyu. West-north-west. 8½ miles.

At this camp I was attacked with a fierce fever, the result of our march through the swamps, brakes, and unhealthy flats of the coast region. 3000 feet above sea.

December 15th:

At 1 p.m. we began our march across the forbidding desert of the Bitter Water. Marenga Mkali, The Bitter Water, is to be found at Chunyu. It has a nitrous taste, and is considered fatal to Zanzibar asses, though cattle are now numerous on the slopes of Chunyu, and the summits of the hilly chain above. The heat was intense, the earth fervid, the thorny jungle a constant impediment, and a sore trouble, and its exhalations nauseating. Had an enemy lurked in the jungle of sufficient audacity and power to withstand a few Snyders, the Expedition might have been ruined there and then, but a kind Providence watched over us and permitted us to straggle into camp, a wretched and almost demoralized caravan. I had taken the precaution to carry 100 gallons of water with me, half of which but wetted the lips of men and animals. That night bivouacked under a wide spreading and proud baobab, scarred with the knives of more than half a thousand caravans.

December 16th:

Continuation of our march across the Marenga Mkali and arrival at Ugogo—17½ miles.

Added to the torments of great thirst, and heat, both Frank Pocock and I suffered from fever. It was useless to fight against the inevitable. As the men could not be urged to keep rank and order on such a march, and as the white men and I were disabled by sickness and heat from assuming the command, the men were permitted to march as they best could while we hoped and prayed that neither casualties nor loss would follow such a disorganised proceeding; when near the confines of Ugogo, we met the natives hurrying to the jungle with gourds full of water for sale, which were eagerly bought up by the thirsty bands, who trudged on sore and distressed from heat and thirst. Many a gourd full of water was purchased for two yards of cloth on this day.

December 17th:

In Camp at Chikombo, Ugogo.

From camp we have a view of a brown plain and browny white hills half denuded of soil. The plain is bleak and bare though many a lofty and noble baobab rears its tremendous stem and globular crown of leafy branches above it. Here and there the square *tembes* [*houses*] of the natives surrounded by idle groups of natives and a few herds of cattle are seen. At various distances from us rise a few hills, and even mountains, but to the feverish eye of the traveller who has but lately suffered from fever, the atmosphere of Ugogo is not pleasant. He looks at everything with a jaundiced eye, and long will remember the bitterness of marching through the land and regard it as the most unlovable country in Africa. The cold winds, chilly atmosphere, feverish feeling, the extortion of the natives, their unwhipped insolence, all combine to render Ugogo hateful to the eye and bitter to the mind.

December 18th:

Chikombo.

The Pocock brothers are both ill of fever. I rose from my sick bed to meet foolish old Mobokoli, Chief of Chikombo, and pay him 9 *doti honga* [*9 measures of cloth as transit tribute*].

December 19th:

Itumbi, Sultan Mpamira. West-north-west $1\frac{1}{4}$ hours. $2\frac{3}{4}$ miles.

Large masses of fine grained granite about this neighbourhood. The Newfoundland Nero is blind and weak from disease.

December 20th:

Leehumwa. West 6 miles. 3700 feet above sea.

Mpamira of Itumbi desirous of enriching himself at our expense was extremely loth to part with us, but consented to our departure on payment of 12 *doti* as tribute to his greatness, which though exorbitant we were glad to pay to be rid of him and his accursed, and uninteresting, country.

Nero, the Newfoundland dog, was despatched today. We arrived at Leehumwa under a very hot sun. Thermometer ranging from 96° upwards in my tent. After being an hour in camp, the sky as has been usual since entering Ugogo became suddenly overcast, the weather became cold, the thermometer descending to 69°. Thunder and vivid lightning preceded a copious rain, and half an hour afterwards the sandy stream bed became filled with an impetuous torrent flowing north by west —probably towards the Pangani. It subsided as quickly as it arose and by night a thin stream alone remained of the torrent.

December 21st:

Halt at Leehumwa.

One of the Chief's sons had died the day previous to our arrival, consequently another halt was necessary until he should finish his examination into the causes which led to the death of his son. The war cry was also heard calling the natives to arms to repel the attack of the predatory Wahaha on their cattle. On our road hither we came across a calcareous *tufa* of the colour of a dirty grey putty in process of formation. It was about a quarter of a mile square, and the accretions resembled very much as if a mixture of very fine sand, lime and alkali had been boiled and poured out, and had hence become congealed. On either side of us rose hills denuded of soil presenting most picturesque views. Some consisted of upright masses of quartz tinted yellow by the presence of iron and exposure to weather.

December 22nd:

Dudoma. 7 miles West by North ½ North. 3825 above sea.

This northern route through Ugogo is as difficult to march quickly through as the more southern routes. We are not subjected to such heavy charges or tributes, but the Chiefs are more numerous, which equalize the expense finally. These defer receiving tribute until the last moment, as being more suitable to their dignity. Our accustomed hour of beginning the march generally finds us here prepared to barter with the cunning and avarice of the native Chief. The Chief of Dudoma is a one-eyed man of forty or thereabouts who having been as far as Mbwenni Pangani fancies himself a great traveller. This unusual commerce with the coast has however not mitigated his avarice, but rather kindled it, as he aspires after richer clothes than are commonly bestowed upon natives . . .

From Dudoma, which is situated on a flat terrace at the base of a range of hills, we obtain a fine view of the far Wahumba country extending like a sea to the north . . .

December 23rd:

Halt at Dudoma.

We had intended to have been most expeditious in settling the *honga* of this Chief this morning, but urgent as we were and ready to meet any reasonable demands, we were not able to close the vexatious affair until evening, when it was too late to think of seeking a new diplomatic antagonist in another Chief. Rain has again set in as it has each day since leaving the coast.

Our ransom was fixed at 18 *doti*.

December 24th:

Zingeh. 8 miles.

From Dudoma we moved first to Mivitikira; Chief Mapokera, who though but two miles from Dudoma, exacted a tribute of 10 *doti*. Thence continuing our march we travelled through a dense bush clothing a slightly elevated ridge, from which after a couple of hours we emerged amid a terrific rainstorm in view of the basin of Zingeh which as we looked at it from under our rain-dripping helmets seemed a lake. Descending into the plain we found it half submerged and brawling streams of yellow water rushing towards the north.

At Dudoma last night a hyaena broke into camp and killed a young man.

December 25th:

Zingeh. Halt.

A more cheerless Christmas was seldom passed by me, and I venture to say that none of the other European members of the Expedition ever experienced such dull, gloomy misery as they did at Zingeh. The weather was chilly, and the sky dripped rain interminably, outside our tents nothing was heard save the patter of rain, and the monotonous chant of some bechilled soldier. Inside the tent was a ground flour reduced to brown paste, the dogs snarled at one another for a bit of a box to seat themselves from the mire, the tent walls draggled as if in sympathy with the everlasting gloom outside. Besides, our men suffered from sore famine—as two yards of cloth purchased here only as much as a palm's breadth of cloth would have procured in Nguru.

December 26th:

Camp at Jiweni or Granite Boulders. 13 miles. Altitude 3151 feet.

On our march to Jiweni passed three streams flowing south. Determined to be rid of Wagogo tribute takers, we struck through a jungle in a west-north-western direction from Zingeh, and by good fortune discovered a path leading through a dense thorny bush, which though it gave us considerable smart and pain, was far preferable to being mulcted daily of large stores of cloth. The old rascal Pembera Mperah was thus left in the lurch as well as his fractious neighbour of Mizanza. The yellow time-tinted boulders which rise majestically above our camp will outlast any chieftain in Ugogo yet. Once this site was a village, and the lowlands southward cultivated fields. Whence this change? Why has friendly Nature reasserted her rights to her earth? What kind of a history would relate the change? Be sure there might be a bloody page inscribed, had a history been written. On these granite grinding stones [*for grinding corn*], into whose faces the grinders have ploughed their tasks deeply, we are told of a few generations who have been here, and are no more.

December 27th:

Kitalalo, Ugogo. West-north-west. 8¼ miles.

During our march the thorny bush continued. The stream Mdaburu was crossed, running a southerly course. Its water was brackish and nitrous. Tracks of elephants were numerous, as well as of other large game. The shrubs and trees were acacias, tamarisks, mimosa, and blue gum. Some luscious tamarinds were found on the Mdaburu. . . .

The sole Somali, Mohammed, a lad from Aden, deserted us on this march. It had been evident for some time that he disliked his position, for he would perform no work, and managed to evade his allotted tasks by some fresh excuse plausibly told. He was accustomed to retire from observation, and in silence nurse his mal-humour and sulkiness, as if there were no other object in life worth living for. As we left camp he left his clothes behind, refusing even to carry his own property, and soon after left my pistol holster in the road. As the rearguard came up, they discovered Mohammed sitting behind a tree alone, while the Expedition was far ahead. Urged to continue the march in their care, he proceeded a mile or so, then slipt into the jungle. Search was made for him in all directions by ten stout fellows, but he was not found.

December 28th:

Halt at Kitalalo, Ugogo. 2775 feet above sea.

Masumami, the Chief, is a fine looking specimen of an African savage. Tall and strongly made, features agreeable, added to his native kindliness of manner and liberality, caused me to be much prepossessed in his favour. He presented me with a fat ox, and a couple of gallons of milk, a most unusual thing for a Mgogo Chief. In return I paid 13½ *doti honga*. Masumami begged most earnestly for poison to kill the people of his ferocious neighbour Pembera Mperah, with whom he was on most unfriendly terms, and begged that I would stop rain from falling on his land, that it might become sterile and his people famish. When I expressed my inability to comply with his wishes he was much disappointed, though it did not injure our welcome.

December 29th:

Mukondoku, Ugogo. West by North. Magnetic. 22 miles.

At early daylight on the 29th, guided by Masumami's son,

we emerged from our camp under the *doum* palms of Kitalalo and a short mile brought us to the broad and great Salina. This singular feature of Ugogo stretches from south of Mizanza to Unyangwira Mountains on the north, a length of about 50 miles, and from Kitalalo east to Mukondoku west—a width of 20 miles. A hilly range or plateau wall which we see in our front as we leave Kitalalo extends from Usekke south to Machenche north, is a natural boundary accepted by the natives as separating Ugogo from Uyanzi, or Ukimbu as it is now beginning to be called. A distance of 75 miles north of Machenche the plain and plateau become blended. The trend of the plain is south, it therefore becomes drained by the Rufiji River. The trend of the northern half of the plateau is north, it therefore is drained by the Nyanza [*L. Victoria*]. Our march across the Salina [*level as a sea, sterile and ungrateful as a desert, Stanley elsewhere remarks*] was most fatiguing. Not a drop of drinking water was discovered en-route, though towards the latter part of the march, a grateful rain shower fell which revived us a little, by parching [*sic*] our thirst, but converted the plain into a quagmire.

December 30th:

Halt at Mukondoku.

On approaching Mukondoku district, which contains over hundred villages, we discovered the Wagogo advancing upon us on the trot, in many sections, with uplifted spears and noisy show of war. This belligerent exhibition however did not much disturb our equanimity, as we were strangers and had given no cause for war, and after exhibiting their prowess by a few boasts and frantic actions, they soon subsided into a more pacific demeanour and allowed us to proceed quietly to our camp under a towering baobab near the King's village.

Five men deserted yesterday, abstracting two guns. This constant desertion from the Expedition compelled me to change my intended route and strike north from Mukondoku instead of proceeding to the Nyanza via Kirurumo. A conspiracy was now discovered by which over 50 men had agreed to desert as soon as we should arrive in the neighbourhood of Jiweh la Singa. The ringleaders were clapped in chains and flogged.

December 31st:

Halt at Mukondoku.

The King's name is Chalula, who is a brother of Masumami of Kitalalo. We paid 24 *doti honga* to him. He, unlike his nobler brother, is a crafty and unscrupulous person, and levies tribute on travellers. His people are numerous, strong and bold, and share the pride and overbearing manner of the King and are prone to insolence and hostility upon the slightest provocation. To strive by force with such a powerful King would require 500 Wangwana armed with Snyders or other superior arms, as Chalula could readily muster 2000 warriors. He is detested by his neighbours . . .

I had great difficulty in keeping my camp clear of the obstreperous mob of Wagogo and was put in no little danger of my life by driving them out.

I had 20 men on the sick list, principally from fever, sore feet, and rheumatism.

The Europeans are well, but are of little use to me as they are frequently sick, though Fred Barker is earnest and assiduous in his duty.

January 1st, 1875:

Mwenna. North 8½ miles from Mukondoku.

From Mukondoku we journeyed by compass north through the great plains, skirting the plateau wall already described, on its eastern side. We passed by several humble Wahumba villages, which though humble, own large herds of cattle, goats, sheep, donkeys and dogs. Some of the young women were very pretty, with regular features, well formed noses, thin lips and graceful forms. Though these villages lay not far from the Unyanyembe [*Tabora*] road, we Europeans were as great a wonder and curiosity to them as though they lived hundreds of miles away. They all desired us to stop and several handsome young fellows wished to go through the process of blood-brotherhood with us. Young Keelusu, the son of the Chief of Mwenna, a tall good looking youth, came to my tent at night and begged me to accept a gift of friendship from him, which was a gallon of new milk yet warm from the udder. Such a welcome present was readily accepted and Keelusu's heart was gladdened with a gold bracelet with a huge green crystal set in the centre, a briarwood pipe, a gilt chain and a regal Sohari cloth, with which gifts he was so overjoyed as almost to weep. His emotions of gratitude were visible in the glistening and dilated eyes and felt in the fervent grasp with which he held my hand. By some magic art on his slippers, he invoked success on my journey and health and well being. The right slipper turned up three times in succession, which was considered to be a good omen.

Though deserted by the guides engaged at Mukondoku, the Expedition advanced 10 *miles to Mtiwi* (*altitude* 2825 *feet*).

January 4th:

Camp on edge of plateau. Altitude 3800 feet. 950 feet higher than our camp at Mtiwi and the great plain. Distance travelled 6 miles.

During the night, we were visited by a tremendous rain storm, during which the floodgates of Heaven seemed literally broken. In an hour six inches of water covered our camp and a slow current ran southerly. Everyone in the camp was distressed in some way. Even we Europeans, lodged superior to our men, were not exempted. The tent walls enclosed a little lake, banked by boxes of stores, and ammunition. Hearing cries outside, I lit a candle and my astonishment was great when I perceived that my bed was an island, with the water threatening to carry me off south with the flow. My shoes were become barks floating on a turbid tide. My guns lashed to the centre tent pole were stock deep in water. But the most comical sight was presented by Jack and Bull, perched on the top of an ammunition case, butting each other rearward, snarling and growling for that scant portion of comfort. In the morning I discovered my fatigue cap several yards outside the camp and one of my boots was sailing steadily south towards the Rufiji when recovered. The harmonium, a present for Mtesa, a good deal of gunpowder, tea, rice and sugar were destroyed. Vengeance had indeed overtaken us. At 10 a.m. the sun came out, astonished no doubt at a new lake formed in one night. By noon the ground was dry enough to permit marching, so with glad hearts we struck west and surmounted the plateau of

Uyanzi, and from our camp looked down upon the spacious plain beneath, and the vast broad region of sterility and thorn we had known as inhospitable Ugogo. A farewell to it, a lasting farewell to it, until some generous and opulent philanthropist shall permit me or some other to lead a force for the suppression of this stumbling block to commerce with Central Africa. This pleasant task and none other could ever induce me to return to Ugogo.

January 5th:

Muhalala, Ugogo. 7 miles North-west by West. 3800 feet above sea.

On this plateau which we now traverse, we have arrived at an elevation which considerably alters the character of the vegetation. On the plains of Ugogo flourished the dwarf bush, a mongrel variety of the noble trees growing on the plateau, consisting of acacia, mimosa, rank-smelling gum trees and *euphorbiae*. Here we have the stately *myombo*, the ash of Africa, as useful for human purposes almost as its European type. The *myombo* grows on ridges, lofty uplands, and flourishes best in a loose brown soil. It utterly rejects the fat alluvium as well as the sandy loam. Where the *myombo* is seen, we may be sure that not far off, strange freaks of rocks will be visible in the bosom of the forest. Gigantic square blocks of the magnitude of cottages, and indeed at a distance resembling human dwellings. Large sheets of iron haematite and gneiss, denuded of soil are also characteristic of this plateau, while still another feature is the succession of ridges or land waves.

On our road to Muhalala, we met hundreds of fugitives hurrying from the battle grounds near Kirurumo, the natives of which were being punished for their adherence to that famous robber Mirambo, by Nyungu, son of Mkasiwa of Unyanyembe.

January 6th:

Camp at Ziwani. 9 miles. West ½ North. 4350 feet above sea.

It required all my patience and tact to march from Muhalala without trouble of a very serious kind. The Wagogo guides hired at Mtiwi had treated us in a similar manner that their treacherous countrymen of Mukondoku had. The Mkimbu chief thought he deserved as much cloth as the powerful Malewa [*Lord of Mtiwi*], and he was not brought to his senses until I appeared before his *tembe* with 12 Snyders, insisting that he lower his pretensions to a reasonable degree. We finally agreed and further hired other guides from him and paid the cloth in advance.

Ascending a ridge whose face was rough with many a block of iron ore and a scabby grey rock on which torrents and rain had worked wonderful changes, within two hours we arrived at Kashongwa, a village situated on the verge of a trackless wild, peopled by a mixture of Wasukuma, Wangwana and Wanyamwezi. Here we were informed by officious Wangwana who seemed glad to meet their friends of Zanzibar, that we were but two days march from Urimi. We did not stay here, as we thought we had lost sufficient time in Ugogo, and had sufficient provisions if our guides and the people of Kashongwa spoke the truth, but continued our journey a couple of hours, and camped near a small pool of water, or Ziwani.

January 7th:

Camp at Ziwani. 10 miles North-north-west. 4350 feet above sea.

In the morning we struck over a level plain covered with dense bush towards the north-west. The path was but ill-defined as few travellers journeyed to Urimi, but the guide who was a native of Zanzibar, was sure he said of his road. In this dense bush there was not a single tree of any great size; it was one vast carpet of bush tall enough to permit us to battle our way among the lower branches, which were so interwoven with one another that it sickens me almost to write of it. Though our march was but 10 miles, it cost us many an hour of labour, of elbowing and thrusting our way to the injury of our bodies and detriment of clothing.

January 8th:

Camp at Ziwani. North by West. 14 miles. 4550 feet above the sea.

We should have reached Urimi on this day had there been any truth in what the villagers of Kashongwa reported, but though we have marched 14 miles, we see no limit to this immense bush, in which I fear to think we are all but lost. Our labours were increased today twofold. Our guide lost the path early in the day, and was innocently leading us in an easterly direction, until I took upon me the part of guide with the aid of a compass. The responsibility of leading a half-starved force of 300 men through a bush one knew not whither made me almost shrink from the task, but there was no help for it. Far better to struggle on in a northerly direction than travel east, when my common sense informed me no relief could issue from that direction. Our rations with which we had been provided are utterly consumed, but the people, poor souls, have held out wonderfully. In the midst of doubt and despair, we came to a large tree, which I caused one of the men to climb with the guide to see if he recognised any familiar feature in the dreary landscape. After a minute examination, the guide declared he saw a ridge not far off to the north, where the village of Uveriveri [*or Were-Were*], was situated. This stimulated our men to new exertions, and by night we arrived at a large pool. I waited anxiously for the rearguard to arrive and ordered guns to be fired and the bugle to be sounded from time to time for their guidance, as without such none could find their way to camp through that pathless terrible bush. At 9 p.m. the rearguard came in, reporting that 5 men and a donkey with a load of coffee were lost in the jungle, and one of the rearguard, one of the most faithful of men, had been detailed by the Captain Manwa Sera to bring up two or three sick who were still behind.

January 9th:

Uveriveri. 2½ miles North by East. 4600 feet above sea.

This was news of a sad serious nature. So many men absent from the camp, and each hour of our stay in the jungle adding to our distress. To stay in this dreary wilderness to hunt missing men was to increase the horrors of our situation and to kill many of those still left. These facts well thought of by me, I ordered the march and continued the journey to Uveri-veri, which we reached after an hour's march. We might as well however have been in the jungle as to have arrived here, for only two families dwelt here, and they had not a grain to spare. In this perplexing situation after obtaining the necessary information I resolved to stay here, and despatched 20 of the strongest men to Urimi, which we learned to be still two long days' journey off, with cloth to purchase food, and 20 others strengthened by food from the medical stores to hunt up the missing men, or at least to ascertain their fate. Late in the afternoon the searchers for the lost returned with the news that they were all dead. One after another had struggled on and on until they had all dropped down to die of sheer fatigue and starvation.

January 10*th:*

Halt at Uveriveri.

With the prospect of starvation impending over us, we were at various expedients until the food purveyors should return. I have roamed the forest miles and miles around and have discovered no game. Others have industriously wandered about in search of mushrooms and edible roots. Others have examined trees to see what they would furnish for food. Some have satisfied their hunger on a dead elephant and have been punished for it with nausea and sickness. In the meanwhile I examined my medical stores, and found to my great joy that I had sufficient oatmeal to give every soul two meals of gruel. An iron trunk was emptied of its contents at once, and filled with 25 gallons of water into which was put 10 pounds of oatmeal and four tins of *Revalenta Arabica*. How I joyed to see the pinched faces lighting up at the prospect of warm nutritious food, how the men gathered round, to tend the fire and stir the porridge, how they watched lest some calamity would happen to it, with what inexpressible satisfaction they drank it and with what fervour they thanked God for His mercy!

At 9 p.m. we heard the sound of a gunshot in the north which announced to us that the food purveyors were not far off, and with this measure of joy we slept content.

A party of hunters searching for food came across a lion's den of which they robbed the two whelps male and female which they brought to me.

January 11*th:*

Camp at Jiweni or The Rocks. North ½ West. 7½ miles. 4850 feet above sea.

The purveyors despatched to Urimi to purchase food, returned this morning with a supply of millet seed just sufficient to give all hands a small meal. Two of them had deserted, which made us poorer in food than we had hoped.

An afternoon march was ordered, while I preceded the caravan to hunt game. I only succeeded in shooting a wild boar and a duck, but these were not despised by the famished people, though it was against their faith to eat pork, being Moslems. This part of the country at this season is singularly devoid of game, though tracks of old date are numerous. The bush usurps every space, so that animals can find no nourishment.

Our camp is however situated at the base of a rocky hill 125 feet high and overlooking a green grassy plain which stretches far towards the north.

January 12th:

Suna, Urimi. 20 miles march. North-east $\frac{1}{2}$ North. 4975 feet altitude.

From Jiweni was a very long and trying march to Suna, along a plain, thence along a thin bush which continued as far as Urimi. The plain may well be called the Elephant Plain from the numerous tracks, even recent, which intersect in every direction. Tired and famished we arrived on the edge of the cultivated fields which begin Urimi, where we at once established a strong camp, whence we had a view of the Jiweni or Rocks where we had rested the day before, as they were the only eminences visible above the ocean of bush we had left behind us.

January 13th:

Halt at Suna, Urimi.

There was a strange and peculiar air of discontent foreshadowing trouble among the natives of this country when we first emerged from the bush. They did not seem to understand us. They hurried their wives, children and cattle away, deserted the villages, and hovered round our camp menacingly, carrying in their hands a prodigious quantity of arms. In the morning trouble seemed very near. To prevent this if possible, I called out to the natives to come to the camp. A few of the boldest advanced and sat down, to whom I disclosed the nature of our Expedition frankly and candidly and whom I furnished with gifts to their Chief as an expression of our good will and friendship. But nothing seemed to avail until I heard that some of my men led by famine had robbed the food from several villagers, when being told by the natives that such report was true, I [had] the culprits seized and punished before them, and the value of the food stolen paid in full. By this means confidence and tranquility was restored, and a friendly commerce at once established between the natives and the men of the Expedition.

January 14*th:*

Halt at Suna, Urimi.

The Warimi are the finest natives we have encountered between here and the sea. They are robust, tall, manly in bearing and have very regular features. The nose is not flat, though broad at the base, the mouth is not overlarge but well shaped. For the first time also we have met naked people, for the men have not the slightest shred of cloth or blade of grass to hide their nakedness.

The married women alone are distinguished by dress of any kind. The men are all circumcised, affect brass wire cinctures, armlets and leglets and brass wire collars; beads decorate the hair and a pile of necklaces encircle the neck. The war costumes were curious and various which they put on when war seemed imminent with us, feathers of kite and hawk, mane of zebra and giraffe surrounded the head, while their bodies were smeared with ochre, chalk and fat, presenting a hideous and disgusting appearance. The women I thought slightly fairer in colour than the men. I did not see one flat foot or thick lip in the district, though they had all the negroid wool. Their heads were mostly shaved, except what hair was left in thin wavy lines near the forehead.

Their arms consisted of spears, and long powerful bows, and yard long arrows, and shields of rhinoceros hide . . .

They recognize no chief, except elders and the principal fighting-men. I saw one native nearly 7 feet high . . .

January 16*th:*

Halt at Suna, Urimi.

This morning I mustered the force of the Expedition that I might see what losses had been incurred since leaving the coast.

Number of men left the coast: 347

Present	Left behind sick	Dead	Deserted
230	8	20	89

Only 230 out of 347! 117 men missing. Those 89 deserters mean to me a loss of about $2000 advance [*paid to the men at the outset*] and a weakening of my force which I cannot restore.

The people improved rapidly during our stay at Suna and had we been in a land where there was abundance and perfect confidence, I should have halted longer to establish their strength, but I have noticed growing symptoms of discontent among the natives and it is necessary we should march before open war manifests itself. Ted Pocock has been seriously ill since we have arrived here, whether it is small-pox, typhus, typhoid or African fever that he is suffering from I know not. He has been wandering in his head the last two days, but I hope sincerely that he will recover as he has been very useful to the Expedition. He is a young man of such cheerful disposition that his loss would be seriously felt.

January 17*th:*

Chiwyu. 5 miles North-north-west $\frac{1}{2}$ North.

As we left Suna with which we were all heartily tired for we all lived in doubt and suspicion, hundreds of naked natives came to stare at us for the last time. We left one man behind sick of dysentery which has been the curse of this Expedition.

Ted Pocock was put into a hammock at 8 a.m. As he felt the easy contrast between the hammock and his hard bed under the boat, he said "Ah! This is comfortable". Except for extreme debility he did not seem specially bad, though I was struck with the quiet and ominous stillness of his form compared with the uneasy restlessness of the previous days. Last night as he was sponged in cold water, I noticed about a hundred red pimples with white tops scattered over his chest and arms. A few were so like small-pox pustules that I was led to believe that Ted was suffering from a mild case of small-pox.

Conveyed on the shoulders of four stout men, and attended assiduously by his brother Frank, I heard no more from him except from Frank who remarked to me that Ted had once exclaimed that "His master had just hit the right place," and I fancied he was doing well, but arriving at camp at 10 a.m., I was summoned to the sick man's hammock and reached it only in time to see the young man breathe his last. Poor Pocock was dead! God rest his soul. He was a gentle, amiable creature, of medium stature, shy blue eyes and a light coloured, silky hair. He was excessively fond of his brother, and did his duty in my employ well and efficiently, and was always civil. His brother Frank possesses these virtues perhaps in a greater degree than his brother Ted, but it would have been difficult to elect two better young men for the African Expedition than Francis and Edward Pocock.

We buried Ted by night under a stunted *myombo* tree, deeply marked with a cross. May he rest in peace in this grave, having lived to drink of the extreme southern sources of the Nile.

Fred Barker is also very feeble, and I have a fever, but I performed the burial service over my departed companion.

Advancing 36 miles at an altitude close on 5000 feet, the Expedition penetrated into the district of Ituru where the natives spoke a different language from any hitherto encountered and as they stand about camp gaping curiously, employ themselves in plucking the hair from their faces and armpits, idly leaning on each others' shoulders. *Stanley listed the principal ailments of his men as dysentery, ophthalmia, rheumatism, sciatica, asthma, spasmodic affection of the chest, swollen legs and diseases of the skin.*

January 21*st:*

Vinyata, Ituru. 4900 feet above sea.

My men continue to drop off most mysteriously; Kaif Halleck, the letter bearer to Livingstone on my Expedition of 1871, was left behind suffering from asthma and I have three other hopeless cases, besides 10 on the sick list. I despatched 5 men to Mangura [*the previous halt*], to bring Kaif Halleck to camp, but they returned unsuccessfully.

At 2 p.m. we broke camp and started northwards attended by several hundred natives. As we arrived in the valley of

Vinyata the people deserted their village in a body, but after we had selected our camp near a wood which lay between us and Mgongo Tembo, they were finally persuaded to return.

January 22nd:

Halt at Vinyata.

Reduced to scant numbers by disease, death and desertion, I felt it incumbent on me to take advantage of the halt this day to make each box somewhat heavier and to discard everything I could possibly do without, and accordingly the next morning after our arrival set about it with all despatch. Half a dozen men were also sent back to hunt up the missing man Kaif Halleck. At night they returned with the news that they had found his body hacked to pieces near Mangura. During the day the Magic Doctor of Vinyata came to camp with a fine fat ox, as a present, but it was evident that he expected to be well paid for it as he commenced to beg for a score of things. As far as reasonable his demands were complied with and the heart of the beast at his request was returned to him. He promised to return in the afternoon to receive his present, but a heavy rain prevented his coming. There was considerable trading between ourselves and the natives and most friendly has been our intercourse.

January 23rd:

Halt at Vinyata, Ituru.

We had intended to have continued our journey today, but the Magic Doctor had not yet obtained his cloth. However at 9 a.m. he came bringing with him a large pot full of curdled milk as a further present. He was then given cloth and beads to the value of two oxen, with which he declared himself perfectly satisfied. Half an hour after his departure the war-cry was heard but imagining that it was to rally the people for war with their neighbours of Izanjeh, with whom we heard they had a quarrel, we paid no particular heed to it until we saw some cleared ground in the vicinity of our camp occupied by a large force of natives. I sent a message to ask them if their quarrel was with us, and if so upon what grounds. To which they replied that some of our men had stolen milk and grain during the night, and that they must be paid for it, otherwise they would fight. The messenger was again sent to them to say that if they would name the cost of the articles stolen, I would pay them and punish the thieves. They named the number of yards required, which were at once given them and they expressed themselves perfectly satisfied.

Five minutes after, two of my men gone to cut wood were attacked, one was killed—young Sulieman—the other narrowly escaped with a few flesh wounds of spear and knobstick. About the same time as we received this news, they made a simultaneous rush upon the camp, discharging arrows and throwing their spears. The men hitherto restrained by me were then ordered to go out and meet them and our first battle with the natives was commenced. The enemy driven and chased from the vicinity of the camp, allowed us to strengthen our defences, which we did with all the speed and despatch in our power, so that in two hours we were prepared to defend the camp against all the natives of Ituru. Meanwhile our men had behaved splendidly and had chased them miles away, and on return each brought a store of grain and food. Later in the day the natives gathered on the tops of their *tembes*, but a lucky shot at 1200 yards distance left us unmolested for the day. Loss to the enemy 6 killed.

January 24th:

Halt at Vinyata, Ituru.

We waited patiently the morning after the battle that we might know what the natives further meditated or whether they repented of their folly in attacking a strong peaceful caravan. We had hopes that they had experienced enough of war, but at 9 a.m. our camp was surrounded by a much larger force than that of the preceding day. They shouted derisively at us inviting us out.

As they began to attack us, I mustered 40 men and divided them into four detachments under their respective Captains and gave them instructions, each detachment by itself, but yet close enough to each other to give aid if necessity demanded it. They were to drive the natives from the plain, procure food and cattle and burn all the villages.

Farjalla, the Captain of the first detachment, mistook utterly my directions. He led his men too far to the left, entered a swampy plain north of the Mwaru River and he and his detachment were killed to a man. Fresh from the scene of the slaughter, the natives bounded confidently towards the second detachment under Ferahan. But Ferahan was a sturdy leader who had some crack shots with him to whom their Snyders were faithful and the enemy met a decisive check.

One youth, Murabo, a lad of 19, whom I had kept in chains for a month for conspiring to desert, and released on this day at his own urgent request, distinguished himself in a remarkable manner. He endeavoured to rescue a wounded comrade but was attacked by too great numbers to fight alone in the open. Keeping his Snyder pointed at the foe, he retreated slowly to a small *boma* which he entered and barred after him and alone defended it fatally until a rescue of 15 men fresh from camp. Ferahan the leader received a spear in his side, but plucking it out, he shot his foe dead and managed to reach the side of young Murabo, who was defending his *boma* single handed. This detachment behaved exceedingly well and killed great numbers, but had not the rescue arrived in time, I doubt whether any of them would have been left alive.

Chakanja, the leader of the third detachment no sooner had marched out of our camp, than he forgot my instructions and continued on his way blindly until he had quitted the valley of Vinyata and had entered peaceful territory. Five of his men with better sense than their leader possessed, allied themselves to Safeni, the leader of the fourth detachment, whose services were most efficient and signal. From the camp he marched his men straight as directed, and by accident came to the *boma* of the treacherous Magic Doctor to which the men rushed with fury, dispersed the people and set fire to the village, capturing eight head of cattle besides fowls and grain. Hence they marched triumphantly in good order, burning every village they came to. In the evening I mustered the fighting men and discovered 21 absent, not one of whom ever turned up again.

January 25th:

Halt at Vinyata, Ituru.

We waited again this day until 9 a.m., that we might know whether the Wanyaturu had fighting enough. As none came with the usual defiant gesture in the neighbourhood of the camp,

I thought it my duty to seal our victory with a fresh display of force. Forty men were accordingly chosen to march in compact order under Manwa Sera to the extremest limits of the valley and burn all villages that were left standing and bring in enough grain and other food to last a week.

My orders were implicitly obeyed and every house and *boma* committed to the flames. Besides such abundance of grain was procured that every man in the Expedition was furnished with 6 days ample provision. A feeble demonstration was made by the enemy but once this day, a single volley however dispersed them. Meanwhile I prepared the baggage for departure and discarded every article that was not actually needed. Our losses were 21 men, 18 guns and 2 revolvers; that of the enemy was assured at 35 dead, besides many seen seriously wounded.

January 26th:

Camp in Forest. 15 miles West.

At 2 a.m. a bright moon shining, the camp was wakened for departure and at 3 a.m. we struck west through the jungle, leaving the Mwaru on our right. By good fortune we were enabled to leave camp with all our baggage, and unmolested we continued on our way until noon, when we selected a strong camp overlooking the Mwaru, whose furious roar re-echoed through the valley which our camp commanded. Our camp was a natural fortress, whose deficiencies were remedied by a palisade and a wall of dense bush piled up against it until it was impregnable against people armed with only bow and spear. We were all glad of a safe night's rest and of a camp where our fevered bodies might cool. Here we mourned the brave dead, talked of their virtues and laughed at the folly of the robber Wanyaturu who had needlessly provoked the vengeance we had inflicted on them.

January 27th:

Camp in Forest. 8½ miles West-north-west.

Fortune certainly favoured us in our march from Ituru, for this morning after half a mile's march we came to the regular road running between Mgongo Tembo and Ituru. The news gladdened every heart and the march was resumed with enthusiasm. We soon came again to the Mwaru, now a river about 20 yards wide and ten feet deep, a volume of water which had we not had our boat and a strong rope would certainly have proved impassable to us. Two sections of the boat were put up and a strong rope lashed to trees on either bank, by the aid of which we crossed the furious stream in safety. After a short pause we made an afternoon's march to a pleasant camp situated on the summit of a commanding ridge from which we saw the hills of Ituru far to the west.

January 29th:

Mgongo Tembo, Iramba. Chief Marewa. North-west 4 miles. 4675 feet above sea.

Continuing our way over the forest-clad ridges and narrow plains we arrived after a march of four miles at the outskirts of the settlement of Mgongo Tembo. We made a halt and sent messengers ahead to announce the arrival of a peaceable caravan, under white men, bound for the Victoria Nyanza. The messengers returned with a native who came to satisfy himself of our peaceful intentions. We were then led to a comfortable camp on the border of a grassy plain a few hundred yards north of the Chief's village. This Chief is a living history and epitome of most of the countries and chiefs in this region. Eighteen years ago he housed Burton and Speke as they journeyed to Unyanyembe. Vexed by his neighbour chiefs he retired to central Iramba, thence after a few years he moved to southern Iramba where he now resides, though proposing shortly to remove again east into the depths of the forest we had just traversed. He is peacefully inclined and friendly to Zanzibar people. Though no warrior, he yet builds strong villages and palisades from before which his enemies are always worsted. Maganga of Rubuga, united with Mirambo, attacked his village three months ago and met his fate, while the robber Chieftain, with whose name mothers still their children's cries and with whose deeds young men are inspired, was compelled to fly.

January 30th:

Halt at Mgongo Tembo, Iramba. East Longitude 34°.37′. 30″. South Latitude 4°.47′.

We soon were friends with Mgongo Tembo [*otherwise Chief*

Marewa, or Elephant's Back from the name of his domain] and gifts were interchanged to our mutual satisfaction. I discovered upon questioning these people that it is the custom of the Wanyaturu to entertain strangers in the way we were entertained; *viz.* with gifts of oxen and then war. If the stranger accedes to their request for the heart of the ox he receives from them, the Magic Doctor extracts certain medicine from it and then urges his people to war against him. If he eats it himself peace is assured. The people of Jiweh la Singa lately made war upon the Wanyaturu, but were worsted and an Arab trader had to abandon his goods in their possession, by which if true, we may consider ourselves as having avenged their losses and made good our own.

"Uneasy lies the head that wears a crown" and though Marewa wears no crown, but is a simple Chief of simple savages, his dignity and authority is envied by many, which compels him to change his sleeping place each night.

January 31st:

Halt at Mgongo Tembo, Iramba.

No sooner are we out of one danger than we are near another.

We have escaped the Wanyaturu, only to find ourselves constantly thinning in numbers, by disease, war and desertion. On mustering the Expedition, I found it numbered only 173 souls. 174 less than the number I led from Bagamoyo. Up to date 77 have died by battle and disease. This is terrible, but God's will be done. My men are still failing me; I have a great number on the sick list. Medicine seems to be of no avail with those suffering from dysentery, only rest, a long rest is needed with abundance of good food. But where in all this region can such be enjoyed? Nowhere. Only on the Nyanza can we hope for such, but the Nyanza is still far and before we reach it many a stout fellow will have been left behind.

Mgongo Tembo is anxious that I should forecast the future for him. He wished to know if he should reap his harvest, if he should have war, how many years he had to live. He has had 16 sons, yet he lamented his failing powers, and wished to be repossessed of his former vigour and strength when he found joy in a multitude of wives and laughed at the ailments of his elders.

Two guides were here hired to take us to Mombiti.

Setting out at daybreak on February 1st, and averaging 9 miles a day, the Expedition moved into the plain of the Luwamberri River which had recently been in flood. Gnu and rhinoceros were seen for the first time, and buffalo, zebra, giraffe, springbuck and waterbuck were incredibly numerous and tame.

February 5th:

Halt in Camp at Mgongo [*a wooded eminence in the centre of the plain*].

Though far removed from any settlement, having found myself misinformed as to the number of days required to traverse the Luwamberri Plain, I was compelled to halt until provisions of grain could be brought from Kituguru, Iramba, a village of three hours distance from camp in a north-east direction. Besides five men had deserted the Expedition between Mgongo Tembo and this camp and to permit such rapid thinning of my already scant numbers without making an effort to capture them would have been unwise, as others might attempt to imitate their example. Ten strong fellows were sent back with instructions to proceed as far as Marewa's to search for the deserters and to bring them dead or alive to camp. Thirty men were also sent to Kituguru with the Wasukuma *pagazis* [*guides*] to purchase food. Meantime I tried my luck at shooting but after hours of fruitless effort I was compelled to return to camp with but a duck and a small antelope as the result of my morning's work. In the afternoon I went to the Mgongo and, tracking a herd of buffalos north, within two hours I came up with an enormous herd numbering about 200. After a tedious scramble and crawl along the ground, I succeeded in getting within 50 yards of a fine animal and in planting a shot near the heart, but the beast after falling managed to rush after the herd. Again tracking them a short distance, I succeeded in getting within five yards of one whom I shot through the shoulder, but he also got away and night by this time closed my unsuccessful hunt.

February 6th:

Camp on Plain near Luwamberri River. 7 miles. 3575 above sea.

At 10 a.m. of the 6th, my detectives returned with three of the runaways, Mkamanga, Saburi Jumbe and Alassi Jumbe. This last had deserted with a box of ammunition and was court martialled. Fifty-one were for hanging him off hand, while 80 pleaded that he should be chained until the termination of the Expedition, and flogged. In the afternoon we made a march, strengthened by the provisions we had purchased at Kituguru, to the Luwamberri River which the aneroid indicated had an elevation of 3575 feet above sea level. The "River" was merely a slight depression running north and south along the plain, marked by a broad growth of papyrus three or four hundred yards wide. The water was about 2 feet deep without a current. During the rainy season however I can readily conceive what a formidable obstacle to travel on this plain this broad—now shallow—river would be. The Wanyamwezi porters related to me how once upon a time a native caravan was entirely lost in the river. Two of the Expedition died while crossing, one a young Msukuma from heart disease, the other Hedi, long sick of chronic dysentery.

During the rainy season the plain resembles a lake and all the animals betake themselves to the Mgongo.

Leaving the plain with its profusion of game and aquatic birds, the Expedition marched another 43 miles and reached Mombiti (altitude 4075 feet) at noon on February 10th. In Mombiti grain was abundant and cheap, 50 pounds selling for 4 yards of cloth.

February 11th:

Halt at Mombiti, Usukuma.

The amount of grain and the number of chickens consumed yesterday and today has been enormous. Visitors from all parts of this populous neighbourhood came to Mombiti with millet, small potatoes, sesamum, tobacco, pot herbs, goats, honey, et cetera, for sale where they found a ready market with our half starved people.

February 12th:

Halt at Mombiti.

I have given two days rest to the wearied people of the Expedition who for their past labours and fidelity have well deserved them. Inordinate eating and festive rejoicings have been the order of the day.

Two roads lead from here to Usiha, one leads through a populous country, the other through a jungle. I prefer the latter as this entire region is disturbed by Mirambo and his robbers, and almost every native is half a robber, such is the condition of lawlessness to which Mirambo's hate to all those who will not recognise him as King has reduced once happy, prosperous, peaceful Usukuma.

February 13th:

Camp in Jungle. 10¾ miles North-east. 3950 feet.

At 6.30 a.m. we made a fair start for the north with 37 additional carriers who had been hired to proceed with us as far as Usiha. I was flattering myself that we were free from all trouble until we reached Usiha, but barely had we been an hour on the march before we were overtaken by messengers from Mitingini, a surly and proud neighbour of Mombiti's Chief who desired to know "Why the White man had gone away without visiting him when he had got ready his village and an abundance of food for our reception and to make brotherhood with the first white man whom he had ever heard of." We rejected the flattering offer with many compliments and a promise that if we returned through Usukuma we would make good our neglect. The messengers would not be satisfied, and we could not return, that being contrary to our principle; and the consequence was 23 of the porters returned. Fortunate indeed was I that I had but engaged them to relieve my tired men otherwise I had been in a dilemma indeed.

February 14th:

Camp Gardner. 9 miles North-east. 2½ miles North-west. 3750 feet.

Perceiving that we were able to march without them, six of the absconding Wasukuma returned and resumed their loads. Gardner the faithful follower of Livingstone's fortunes for nine years, died today of typhoid fever after eleven days illness. He was buried near our camp and the camp has been called after him.

The first lemurs' cries were heard last night.

February 1875

The Expedition crossed the plain of the Monangah River without mishap.

February 17th:

Usiha.

. . . We sent the Guide hired at Mombiti to announce our arrival [*to the people of Usiha*], and request peaceful admission into their country. The villagers received him kindly and said that we might enter their country, as they had no quarrel with anyone save Mirambo. Almost immediately one of the Wanyamwezi donkeys brayed a long and low blast. It would not have been worth mentioning, had it not almost been the cause of war. For Mirambo during his raids hither had a donkey which brayed a similar blast, hence we were regarded as foes. The people flocked out of their cotes fully armed, accoutred and painted for battle and the war-cry was sent pealing through all Usiha. They manned the bushes on each side of us and war was imminent. Ignorant of the cause I happened to step out to the Guide to tell him to inquire what we had done when we had but just entered as peaceful strangers, when all at once the natives came out laughing heartily at the fright they must have given their countrymen, for they were now convinced having seen the white man that we were friends.

February 18th:

Halt at East Usiha.

The wisdom of selecting the jungle road to that of Sanwi and Usanda was made clear this morning, for Mirambo was reported to be not ten miles off, fighting the people of Masari. Not less than 500 warriors visited us during this halt to make sure we were not the terrible Ruga-Ruga the terror of all Usukuma.

February 19th:

Wandui. North 9½ miles. 4125 feet above the sea.

Reinforced by 20 porters from Usiha instead of those who came from Mombiti we set out from southern Usiha attended by some hundreds of curious but friendly natives. We soon came in view of the beautiful and picturesque plateau which now replaces the low hot plain through which we lately travelled. Thickly dotted with massive granite blocks piled up in rugged knolls and hills, or rose up in rounded clumps [*sic*], while between and all around were well cultivated fields, herds of cattle grazing on the short sweet grass—it was a scene of scope and beauty such as we had not met with before, and it made a vivid impression on us all for its novelty and beauty. Villages were numerous, and all surrounded by milkweed hedges leaving lanes to which clung the sweet breath of the cattle whose route to graze lay between them. On approaching the King's village we came to a broad avenue a mile long flanked on each side by a natural wall of massive granite blocks about 50 feet high. At the base of these walls springs sprang on every side, and water trickled along a central drain to the valley below. At the end of the village surmounting rising ground were the King's quarters or villages embowered by patriarchal and wide spreading trees, which rendered the place delightfully cool and agreeable. We did not stay but marched on to Wandui, another territory where the natives leaped for joy to see trading strangers with cloth and beads. No other evidence need be required to show what spirit for commerce animates these people.

February 20th:

Mondo. North ½ West 14½ miles. 3950 feet.

A severe thunderstorm and rain from the north-west took place last night, thoroughly drenching us. Indeed there have been few days since leaving Zanzibar we have not been wetted by rain. Wandui and Usiha are greatly disturbed by fighting factions about them. Masari attacks Usanda, Usanda fights with Masari, and Mirambo battles with both, until the people about them are troubled day and night with the shrill pealing war-cries of the suspicious watchmen. The country still continues beautifully clear and open, rolling in wide waves of rock-crested ridges, and abounds with cattle.

February 21st:

Abaddi, Usukuma. North ½ West. 11 miles. 3975 feet.

Jumah Dipsingessi died today of an overdose of opium [*Discovered in theft on January 28th, he had been flogged and imprisoned in chains.*]

February 22nd:

Halt at Abaddi, Usukuma.

This death of Jumah cost us four *doti* as a fine to the King. The fine was paid to the King's son who came to claim it. The son tried to cheat the King, but being detected was nothing abashed. The Wasukuma like the Waturu are stark naked, though the women wear skins of goats. Herds are numerous, the wide, open, green plateau is whitened by their immense number. The villages are clusters of cone-huts surrounded by manifold hedges of milkweed, through which we find lanes about eight feet wide.

Marching successively through the plateau with its villages, a thorny jungle and a monkey-infested forest, without further affright than a daybreak disturbance caused by some native travellers ringing their globular bells to waken their women to their duties—the sounds were alarming though not inharmonious and could be heard a long distance—*the Expedition covered another* 60 *miles, and on February 27th was rewarded by its first glimpse of Lake Victoria.*

February 27th:

Village of Kagehyi, District of Uchambi, Usukuma. 19 miles. Altitude of Lake varying from 3650 to 3750 by aneroids.

Inspired by the welcome news that this day we should see the Lake which promised to us a long rest from vexatious troubles and marches, we began the march early. Each man marched with vigour. From the summit of a ridge we beheld the Lake at last or a portion of it now known as Speke Gulf, like a broad band of grey cloud lying between a line of cones and hills. The morning was foggy, otherwise it might have presented a scene of great beauty.

After 17 miles march we stood on the line of grey rock hills behind Kagehyi, and as the sun now shone we gazed upon a lake which to the north-west was like a vast sea. To the north and east of us Speke Gulf ran east between the opposing hills of Ukerewe, Usukuma. Magu and Sima Islands dotted the silvery expanse and many a picturesque rock rose white and glistening from its broad bosom.

The native porters banded together and headed by a youthful

Corypheus began an exhilarating song of triumph in honour of our successful march from the Salt Ocean to the great Nyanza in which presently all our men joined, so that the fervid song was heard at Kagehyi. Then gunshots were fired to announce to the wondering people below the arrival of a caravan.

As we marched down the hill in a long procession, the people of Kagehyi marched out to meet us, with spears and bows, with every indication of hostilities, but a few words of explanation converted their hostile minds into friendship and by the time we entered the friendly palisade of Kagehyi situate a hundred yards from the Lake, we had a multitude of men, women and children shouting our welcome to the Nyanza.

February 28th:

Halt at Kagehyi.

This day we dedicated to rest and a feeling of gratitude to Almighty God who has wonderfully preserved us through manifold dangers, from ferocious savages whose fierce hearts thirsted for our blood, from the sickness which has overtaken so many of our fellows, from hunger which has killed numbers of our people. 'Tis true we are much reduced in pride of numbers but thanks to Providence who has watched over us night and day we are still strong to cope with robbers and fractious people, though my prayer is that we meet no more, for to conquer costs many a valuable life. We can barely believe that our long march to this place has terminated, or that we have not tomorrow to brace ourselves for another day's long march. How my weak and sick and wearied men rejoice at the sweet repose before them. They celebrate it with songs and shouts, while I deep in my inmost heart feel nothing but devoutest thanks to my God. Our number is 166, or 181 less than when we started from the Coast. Both Frank Pocock and Fred Barker are well and so am I. May we continue so to the end of our long journey.

PART II

CIRCUMNAVIGATION OF LAKE VICTORIA

March 1st, 1875–May 8th, 1875

CIRCUMNAVIGATION OF LAKE VICTORIA

Arrival at Kagehyi, on the south-eastern shore of Victoria Nyanza, marked the end of the first phase of Stanley's journey. It had lasted 103 days, 70 of which had been marching days. Pedometers recorded the distance covered as 720 statute miles. The average rate of advance had been 7 miles a day inclusive of halts.

The second phase was to be the circumnavigation of the Lake. The first week of March Stanley spent in writing despatches for the sponsors of the Expedition, The Daily Telegraph *and* New York Herald; *in preparing the boat; and in establishing good relations with Kaduma, Chief of Kagehyi, in whose territory the body of the Expedition would remain until the explorer's return.*

March 7th:

Kagehyi.

The boat is completed, and has had a trial on the Nyanza, wherein she gave me satisfaction. Kaduma the Chief has promised to be my guide as far as Moburu in Ururi, for a consideration, but he insists that I wait four days longer that he may make medicine and see what kind of a moon it promises to be. The King of Uchambi Kidana, a boy of ten or thereabouts, has through his elders been fee'd by me. Sungoro, or Mse Saba, who lives here is at present away in Ukerewe where he is building a dhow of 20 or 30 tons burthen.

March 8th:

Igusa.

At 1 p.m. after vainly endeavouring to persuade Kaduma Chief of Kagehyi to accompany me as a guide as far as Ururi, I sailed from Kagehyi with 10 stout sailors of the Expedition in the *Lady Alice*, a cedar boat 24 feet long and 6 feet wide which we have carried in sections from the Coast for the purpose of exploring the Lakes of Central Africa. The men were rather downhearted and rowed reluctantly, as we have had many a grievous prophecy that we shall all drown in the Lake, or die at the hands of some of the ferocious people living

63

on the shores of the Nyanza. To which having no other aid I must say God's will be done. As a precaution against dealing with some tribes, I have loaded the boat with 600 pounds of flour, besides 200 pounds of dried fish. Lutari stands at the eastern end of the Bay of Kagehyi. On rounding the point another bay extending about 20 miles east was seen. At its western end stands Igusa, and its eastern horn is formed by the country of Magu.

March 9th:

Natwari Island at the mouth of the Shimeeyu River.

Having procured a guide called Saramba who knew the country well as far as Ururi, we left Igusa with better prospects before us than we had anticipated. When near the island of Mashakka a storm rose which drove us at a rapid rate. As it was all in our favour, we were able to do a good day's work. Saramba who had never seen anything larger than a 20-foot canoe, exclaimed that if we went on at this rate, we would finish the world before long. At 4 p.m. we sailed by the mouth of the Shimeeyu a mile and a half wide, clothed with several rocky islands. This river receives the Duma from the east, the Luwamberri from the south and the Monangah from the south-west. Arriving at Natwari, a small bush-overgrown island near its mouth, we laid up for the day, quite satisfied with the conduct of the *Lady Alice* during the gale.

March 10th:

At anchor, south of Iramba near coast of Manassa.

Left Natwari Island at 8 a.m., and sailed to a bay which promised to reveal a river, but we found none of any consequence. Passing Mazanza we coasted by the shore of Manassa, and anchored at 4 p.m. after endeavouring to land in the centre of a bay south of Iramba. We had tried to land but were chased away by three hippopotamus who rushed at us open-mouthed. The bay for a considerable distance from shore is very shallow so that these amphibious monsters had the advantage of us.

They rowed eastwards along the southerly shore of Speke Gulf, returning along the northern coast to sail round the large island of Ukerewe. Successive days' entries in the Diary include elegant ttle maps showing the principal features of the coast, the route travelled and the distance accomplished.

March 14th:

Anchored with a stone between the Irangara Islands. Natives amused themselves by asking questions until late in the night and in the morning would fain have continued their interrogation had we not put an end to them by gently sailing away. Low hilly ranges covered with woods mark the coast from Wiru to Irangara.

They then sailed northwards along the coast of Ururi.

March 18th:

Majita Mountain to Dobo.

Ururi populous and well cultivated, country well adapted for cultivation. Majita is conspicuous for its lofty triangular table-top mountain. Slept at Burdett Coutts Island last night. Few islands possess better advantages. The Waruri said that we should be eight years circumnavigating the Lake. The pests of the Lake are the millions of white gnats. Mosquitoes are few, comparatively. Fish black, blue and striped.

March 19th:

Having arrived at anchorage a little after dark we were led last night to seek shelter between some of the outlying rocks of Dobo. We fastened bow and stern, but at midnight a storm arose and drove us against the rocks and we should have been soon smashed irretrievably had not the oars lashed alongside of the boat, fended us off somewhat. Amid a pelting rain, and angry loud sounding waves we managed to get out of danger, and slept in wet clothes.

The two Dobo Islands are uninhabited though they once were peopled . . .

Externally the aspect of these islands is singularly bare, and rugged, but there are spaces covered with green grass, and good soil. The hippos find rich nocturnal pasturages. Iguanas abound here.

Suspecting that an important river emptied itself into the bay of Mori we scudded before the wind at 7 knots but on coming to an island and climbing to the top of the highest peak the formations and bends of the shore were clearly visible. A small river flowed from west of south; beyond south-east is plain bounded by rocky hills. The island at the end of Mori Bay was rich in varied plants, though but a few hundred yards in length. *Euphorbiae Eschinomenae*, with yellow flowers on which birds as yellow as they nourished and darted to nests suspended under the branches—yellow breasts, dim grey backs with a tinge of green at the sides. One had a black beard which from its superior size I take to be the male. Among other plants, lianas, thorns, mimosa, acacia, vines of many species, tall aloetic plants, wild pineapple, cane, spear grass. Crocodiles are numerous.

March 22nd:

Halted last night at Bridge Island so named for possessing a natural bridge of basalt about 20 feet long by 12 feet wide. Under the arch you pass from one side of the island to the other. The island is covered with mangrove trees, whose branches extend far into the water, under which our boat might be screened by their deep shade. The summit of the island is about 50 feet above the lake. If the wind blows strong from one side we may pass round to the other side of the bridge where the boat might rest tranquilly whilst through the arch we might obtain a view of the surge of angry waves. From the summit of the island which is easy of access we obtained a fine view of lofty Ugingo Island and the tall steep mountains of Ugeyeya with the level plain of Wagansu and Wigassi. West is seemingly boundless sea and north distant lands. Scenery of Ugeyeya bold in the extreme, hills on the plains like domes seem tossed up in every direction while the strange island seems to brood in its solitude in the middle of the Lake, surrounded by a waste of waters. An island closely situated to it has a small cave.

March 24th:

Arrived at Muiwanda we found a people speaking a strange language. Though the shore was lined by a multitude, we anchored within an arrow's flight from the shore and began to persuade the natives to bring food to us, by holding out a bunch of beads. They wished us to land. We refused saying we did not know them and they might do us harm, to prevent which, if they required beads they might come to us with provisions in their canoes. Much diplomacy was shown on both sides. Finally trade was opened, and while trading for food I found the people very friendly and disposed to answer all my questions. They spoke the language of Usoga with a slight dialectic difference. Neither men nor women wore anything. save a kirtle of grass, or plaintain leaves which the latter wore. Men had extracted two front teeth of lower jaw, had bracelets of iron rings, rings above elbows and in ears. Shaved their heads in eccentric fashion . . .

March 26th:

. . . Yesterday we left Muiwanda and coasted longshore by the promontory of Chaga or Shaga. When we hesitated about going ashore the natives of Chaga asked: What have you to fear from us who wear no clothes?

At 2 p.m. we arrived at Ngevi Island opposite Kefweh—Chief Kamoydah. As there was a strong south-west breeze driving us ashore we furled sail and anchored. Soon two canoes arrived from mainland to enquire who we were. To this we answered and then proceeded with cat-like progress to persuade them to tell us what lands these were about us. For a necklace of beads we obtained the desired information. We had concluded interrogating them when a larger canoe manned with 15 men came near us. These confiding in numbers were rude and insulting which we bore with patience. After they had ranged alongside, their eyes became [*so*] fired with greed that they could barely restrain their hands. They said they came from the King who desired us to take our boat close to their shore. After seeing the behaviour of his emissaries we persisted in remaining where we were in our snug anchorage under the lee of Ngevi. They then proceeded to brandish long spears—12 feet in length—and took up their targes of twisted reed, but, firing my revolver that they might see what weapons we had, they all but three jumped into the water. We on our side laughed heartily at the cowardice of the valiants. These few shots so crushed their arrogance that they became quite submissive and presented us with bananas, an act of courtesy I did not fail to reward.

March 27th:

Continuation of 26th.

Now fast friends they promised to go ashore to bring abundance of food. While we expected them we perceived the same canoe return with a much larger number of people, and a veritable set of Bacchanalians, of which the Chief or Mukungu was by far the most boisterous. They came to repeat the request of Kamoydah, the King, but we begged to be excused from moving from our present safe anchorage, the waves were rough, the wind was strong. They begged, they implored and all but threatened. Three more canoes now came up loaded with men, and these added their united voices to invite us on the part of the King to his shore. Finding us still obstinate, they laid hands on the boat, and their insolence increased almost to fighting pitch. To put an end to this lest worse might happen to some of us, I accepted the invitation and told them that if they showed me the way I would go with them. A loud howl of delight was the response to this. The anchor was hauled up and the sail was hoisted, and as it blew a gale the sail soon felt the power of the wind, and in a few seconds we were rushing before the gale leaving the discomfited Wagamba in the middle of the angry sea making frantic gestures. We continued on our way for five miles in the direction of Usuguru [*at the north-westerly corner of the Lake*] and then lowered sail and prepared to rough it in the open Lake. At dusk the gale abated and an hour afterwards was a perfect calm, but from the south-east at 8 p.m. blew the most horrible tempest—hailstones as large as filberts, and rain in such torrents that all hands were required to bail the boat out, lest we sank at our anchorage. It lasted an hour, and then we took advantage of a lull to row back to our former place near Ngevi Island where we passed the night in such comfort as wet clothes could furnish us. The next morning we sailed along the coast of Uvira and Usowa, and dropped anchor between Namungi and Wantambi, where we found a people hospitable and good natured.

March 28th:

Passed a troublous night of toil and suffering from rain and hail storm. The boat tossed and pitched and groaned as if each timber was being rent from the sides. In the morning while sailing close to the shore we were stoned by the people. Two great rocks came near to crushing the boat's sides, but a few revolver shots stopped that game. Arriving between the islands of Bugeyeya and Uvuma, we had the misfortune to come across a nest of Lake pirates who make navigation impossible for the Waganda. Ignorant of their character we allowed 13 canoes to range alongside and commenced a friendly conversation with them, but I was soon informed of their character when they made an indiscriminate rush upon the boat. Again I beat them off with my revolver, and having got them a little distance off opened fire with my elephant rifle—with which I smashed three canoes, and killed four men. We continued on our way hence immediately to the Napoleon Channel, and after a look at the great river outflowing northwards [*the Victoria Nile at the Ripon Falls*], sailed to Marida where we rested secure and comfortable.

Stanley now entered the sphere of influence of Mtesa, King of Uganda, to whom he sent messengers announcing his intention to visit the court. Meanwhile he continued to sail westwards along the northern coast of the lake.

April 2nd:

At Beya, I halted to ask the natives who were collecting bananas from the King's gardens the direction of the bay near the King's Capital and I was informed it was but six hours off, west. Continuing our journey we were overtaken about dusk by the Mkama of Buvwa, who led us to a comfortable resting place for the night. This morning was rainy, wet, and chilly and I halted until 10 a.m. then started, but near Kadzi Cave we were met by six large canoes containing 182 men sent by Mtesa to escort us to Usavara where he had a hunting camp. Entreated by them to give the Waganda a rest we halted for the day at Kirudo. Magassa the chief of this party entertained us most royally.

April 3rd:

Starting at 10 a.m. we pulled all in concert, the King's canoes making a fine appearance. At 8 p.m. pulled into a cove near Soweh an island in Murchison Bay.

April 4th:

Arrived at Usavara, the hunting camp of Mtesa. Received at landing by Katekiro, Chief of Budu and 2000 Waganda drawn in two lines, 16 drums beating, musketry firing, conducted to a house whither 10 oxen, 16 sheep and goats, 3 dozen chickens, eggs, bananas, sweet potatoes were sent to feed me and my men. In the afternoon received in state by the Sultan.

Katekiro was not a personal name, but a Court title: Prime Minister, as Stanley discovered.

April 5th:

Halt in Usavara.

As I had read Speke's book for the sake of its geographical information, I retained but a dim remembrance of his description of the court of Uganda. If I remember rightly Speke writes of a youthful prince, vain and heartless, and a wholesale murderer and tyrant delighting in fat women who have been made thus unctuous by being fed on milk. Doubtless Speke described what he saw but it is as far from being true of the state of things now, as white is from black. Indeed I have seen that which, if I had not living witnesses of character unimpeachable, would be set down by Europeans as romance. I have seen in Mtesa King of all Uganda, Usoga, Unyoro, Karagwe, Uzongora, Kamiru and Uwya, a most intelligent, humane and distinguished prince, a man who if aided timely by virtuous philanthropists will yet do more for Central Africa and civilisation what fifty years of gospel teaching unaided by such authority cannot do [*sic*]. I see in him the light that shall lighten the darkness of this benighted region, a prince well worth the most hearty sympathies and evangelical teaching which Europe can give him. In him I see the possible fruition of Livingstone's hopes, for with his aid the civilisation and enlightenment of a vast portion of Central Africa becomes most possible.

I remember the ardour and love with which Livingstone writes of Sekeletu, Chief of the Makololo; had he but seen Mtesa, his love and ardour for Mtesa had been tenfold, and his pen and voice would have been heard calling all good men to his aid. Of all my African experiences, I call my visit to Uganda the most interesting. I found Mtesa, not a tyrannous savage, a wholesale murderer, but a pious Mussulman and an intelligent humane King reigning absolutely over a vast section of Africa, loved more than hated, respected more than feared, of all his subjects.

April 6th:

Halt at Usavara.

I found him powerful over his own country and influential over his neighbours. I saw the turbulent Mankorongo of Usui and the robber chieftain Mirambo through their ambassadors kneel and tender their allegiance to him. I saw over 3000 soldiers of Mtesa nearly half civilised. I saw 100 chiefs who might be reckoned in the same scale as the principal men of Zanzibar or Oman clad in his rich robes, and armed after the same fashion, and witnessed with astonishment order and law such as obtains in half-civilised countries respected.

All this is the result of a poor Mohammedan's labour, Muley bin Salim, who first began teaching the King the Doctrines of Islam. False and contemptible as they are, they are far preferable to the ruthless instincts of a savage despot, whom Speke and Grant left wallowing in the blood of women, and I honour the name of Muley bin Salim, Moslem and slave-trader though he be, who has wrought this happy change. Colonel Grant must have believed Mtesa to be in the same state of ignorance and simplicity that he and Speke left him in 1862, for I saw how much he estimated him by the presentation of a cheap silver medal, of the value of one dollar or so sent by the hand of Colonel Linant de Bellefonds. Had Colonel Grant been present he would have laughed as heartily at his own simplicity as I was amused.

Guided by what I remembered Speke had written of Mtesa's character I had furnished myself with some toys and cheap showy articles, but after an interview with him, I blushed at the insult I came near doing him and to condone for my simplicity I almost impoverished myself to do him honour, and had it been possible would have marched to Egypt to purchase suitable gifts becoming his station and character. Though all Europeans who have yet visited him, Captains Speke, Grant, Colonel Long, myself and Colonel Bellefonds are no ivory traders, but had and have higher aspirations, all our gifts to Mtesa put together have been beggared in value and utility by what Khamis bin Abdullah, a simple ivory trader gave him.

Khamis bin Abdullah, ivory trader and Arab commander, had seconded Muley bin Salim to the court of King Mtesa; the gifts that he conferred were the regenerating truths of Islam.

April 7th:

Halt at Usavara.

I was a witness yesterday of another instance of Mtesa's greatness. Forty canoes with 30 men in each containing near 1200 men rowed races while Mtesa and his 300 wives and upwards of 3000 spectators lined the shore to view the sport. I was called upon to exhibit my prowess in shooting. A young crocodile lay sleeping on a rock about 200 yards from shore, and rowing within 100 yards of it I had the good fortune for the honour and reputation of white men to shoot it. I should not have liked to have attempted the same feat twice running, for I doubt much I could have succeeded. However, to my vanity be it said this act was applauded as another evidence that we Europeans were dead shots. In the afternoon, we exercised at target practice, at which an accident occurred but fortunately without injury to anyone. [*Barker's*] double-barrelled Holland gun Number Eight burst in the hands of Mtesa. On seeing him safe the men rushed up to congratulate him and a goat was slain across the threshold of his residence, in whose blood Mtesa dipped his finger, and signed his forehead with it.

This morning escorted by a fleet of 84 canoes manned by 2500 men, we went to visit Dwaga, his palace during the Ramadan, then to see a dhow in process of construction.

In person Mtesa is tall and slender, with intelligent and agreeable features, large eyes, and not an overlarge mouth. The expression of his face is one of amiability veiled by native dignity, which he assumes when in council, to uphold the name of his station. When not engaged in important affairs, he permits this amiability and his humour full play, which is often accompanied by peals of hearty laughter. He is fond of hearing about courts, and the ways of the European world and is never tired of the wonders of civilisation. He is ambitious to imitate, as much as lies in his power, the ways of the white man. When he is told any piece of information he takes upon himself the task of translating it to his chiefs, though many of them might already have understood what had been said.

April 8*th:*

The court moved from Usavara to Ulagalla the King's Capital. It is sited on the summit of a hill overlooking a great and beautiful district. Great wide roads lead to it from all directions. The widest and principal road is that overlooked from the Durbar [*council chamber*] of the King's Capital. It is about 400 feet wide and nearly 10 miles long, to be made longer. Either side is flanked by the houses and gardens of the principal men.

April 9*th:*

Halt at Ulagalla, the King of Uganda's capital.
Received by the King this morning in such state as outdid the previous exhibition.

April 10*th:*

Halt at Ulagalla.
Mtesa gave me a walking cane. He was very anxious to know what good thing I wanted, to show his regard for me. I answered that he had nothing in all his kingdom I coveted, that I came not to receive but to give. He offered me 20 tusks of ivory which I refused declaring that if he offered me a thousand they would be valueless to me, as I came for a different purpose, that I came to see countries, people, and kings and waters.

April 11*th:*

Halt at Ulagalla.
I have been again fortunate in meeting a white man in the heart of Africa [*the previous one had been Dr. Livingstone*], for M. Linant de Bellefonds, or Abdul Azziz Bey in the service of the Khedive, arrived at the capital today with 40 soldiers. He came in great state which gave Mtesa much delight to see the discipline and order of his advance towards the Capital.

April 12th:

Halt at Ulagalla.

The king gave audience to Linant de Bellefonds. I afterwards dined with the French officer at his house.

April 13th:

Halt at Ulagalla.

Dined with M. Bellefonds who I find is an intelligent traveller and takes much interest in the geographical discoveries now being made between Uganda and Khartoum.

April 14th:

Halt at Ulagalla.

I have warned the King of my intended departure, and he has promised to let me have 30 canoes and men to transport the Expedition from Kagehyi, Usukuma, to the Katonga River [*Uganda*].

April 15th:

Departed from Ulagalla for Usavara where my boat lay. Colonel de Bellefonds accompanied me.

April 16th:

Still at Usavara waiting for the promised canoes, and the Grand Admiral of the fleet, Magassa, a vain youth, but one who understands Kiswahili and has visited Zanzibar. Magassa arrived in the afternoon and was taken to task for delaying me, but he promises everything will be ready for an early morning start tomorrow.

April 17th:

Departed for Camp. Saluted by a volley from a portion of Bellefonds' troops who had escorted us to Usavara. Magassa has but 10 canoes with him out of the 30 as promised but he is confident he will get the remainder at the island of Sesse [*at the north-western corner of the lake*].

April 18th:

I parted with Magassa that he might collect canoes in Sesse. Under escort of two canoes manned by Sentageya and Sentum, soldiers of Mtesa, I continued on my way.

April 21st:

[*Neighbourhood of Sesse Island.*]
Magassa arrived here without success at 8 p.m. having lost two killed. Natives refuse to send their canoes to Usukuma. Magassa however is certain that Magura the Chief Admiral will be with us in a day or two with 14 canoes, the remainder we will pick up at Usongora.

Assured of Mtesa's good will and assistance, Stanley was now anxious to return to Kagehyi as soon as possible, lest the Expedition should break up in his prolonged absence. He sailed south along the western coast of the lake and reached Bumbireh Island.

April 28th:

Leaving our shelter at Barker's Island with a fair wind we sped from the island at a rate of 5 knots. At 9 a.m. came to a small cove on the south-eastern end of Bumbireh—Antari Chief. The precautions and prudence which had formerly governed us in our intercourse with unknown tribes were in this instance omitted, as we had nothing whatever in our boat except a little coffee and fruit-food. Besides, Bumbireh being subject to Mtesa, we feared no evil. As we entered the cove we saw the plateau's summit lined with men, and heard shouts like war-cries, yet necessity and imminent starvation compelled us to ground our boat and endeavour to entice the people to part with some food for us for cloth or beads. As soon as we grounded our boat the men rushed down from the plateau, and as I saw their hostile demeanour I loaded my two guns and revolvers, and told my men to push the boat off, but my people either deemed I was too suspicious, or else their dread of starvation got the better of their fear of man, for they did not stir a hand to obey me, but began to make friendly speeches to the natives who now numbered several score, to say that they were Wangwana, friends of Mtesa come to purchase food.

The natives at this lowered their spears, and advanced towards the boat with smiles and friendly gestures, but as soon as they touched the boat, they dragged her with their united forces far on dry land despite our threats or entreaties. While they were doing this my revolvers were twice aimed at them, but I was each time entreated by my men to be patient, and finding my people so deluded with the idea that we were among friends, I contented myself with sitting in the boat until they were taught by experience that friends never act so outrageously.

The natives increased their numbers rapidly, newcomers were violent drawing their bows until they were bent double close to us, and holding their spears as if they were about to launch them, uttering their war-cries. The Mkama came and a policy of guile and falsehood was adopted. They said since we were friends of Mtesa we should stop on the island until Antari was informed of our arrival. He then said that if we had anything to give him he would be content to receive it. We gave him two cloths and beads and he declared himself satisfied. He then ordered his men to bring him our oars, which they did, and I still irresolute was compelled to yield in quietness. They carried the oars away, and with them the warriors of the Mkama slowly left one by one.

Half an hour afterwards, while I had been bewailing my tameness the Mkama came to the brow of the hill followed by about a hundred and fifty warriors and said he wanted 5 cloths and 5 pieces of wire. We said we had no wire, but we would give him 20 cloths if he returned our oars to us. Upon this he shouted to prepare for war and his people began to descend with drawn bows. I told my men to push the boat into the water, and I began the action with my elephant gun, killing one of the foremost, and wounding another. Before I could lay my hands on my second gun, the boat was in deep water, the men clinging to her sides. Assisting one in I told him to assist the others in while I kept the enemy off with my shotgun loaded with buckshot. This did good service, for they withdrew in haste back to the hills, while my men tore up the boards and seats and used them as paddles with which we got out of the cove then hoisted sail and sailed away still firing at the wretches.

April 29th:

We pulled or paddled and sailed before a slight breeze all night and in the morning found ourselves about 20 miles to the south-east of Battle Cove. Mid-day we had quite a gale lasting an hour which drove us about 8 miles further, then came a perfect calm. Continuing paddling in the direction of the south, we made but slow progress, but at night we found ourselves about 10 miles from an island where we proposed to take shelter if we could reach it. But at 9 p.m. another gale arose which swept us to the south-east past the island, and finding that all our efforts to keep the sail up or to get the boat headed round [*were vain*], we resigned ourselves to what fate had in store for us. In the morning I found that we had drifted about 12 miles to the south-west, and seeing an island about 10 miles to the south-east I urged my people once more to try their paddles.

April 30th:

At noon we came to Refuge Island, and a more woebegone crew could hardly be found. We had now been some 48 hours without a morsel of food, nor it seemed to us was there any prospect of any. But on searching the island we found about a dozen bunches of wild bananas, out of which we made a hearty meal. Here I was struck down with the first fever I suffered on the Lake, the result of rain and water and hunger.

May 1st:

Halted on Refuge Island all day, and feeling better, bestirred myself to make oars by lashing pieces of board to poles which we cut from the island. Though they were but poor substitutes for our ash oars, they promised to be better than paddles. We found some more bananas, and thanked God for even this small mercy.

Oarless they sailed and paddled on through bad weather for another three days.

May 5th:

At early dawn we took a view around, but met nothing but wild waves and distant shores. We ascertained our position to be 10 miles north of Mwanza; Kagehyi bore south-north-east. We sounded and found 310 feet of water. After 9 hours rowing we arrived at Kagehyi to be welcomed by the men of the Expedition. They were such robust fine-looking men that I hardly knew them. The news that I heard on my arrival was very sad. Fred Barker had died on the 23rd April of a congestive chill. He had been enjoying himself tolerably well over a month, when he began to ail, lay in bed, feeble and prostrated. He ate but little, was attacked frequently with aguish fits. On the 22nd he had been out shooting hippopotami, on the 23rd about 9 a.m. he felt another attack of the shivers coming and went to lie down. Frank declares he gave him brandy, heaped bed-clothes on him, but he never warmed, for his blood was congealed and he died. He was buried the same day about 3 p.m. between our hut and the Lake, and a wall of stones surrounding his grave is all that marks his resting place. Besides this sorrowful tidings, Mabruki Speke, Jabiri, and Akida had died of dysentery. Mabruki had followed the fortunes of Burton, Speke and Grant, Livingstone and myself. Could an epitaph be written over his grave: Here lies the most faithful and true servant.

Stanley estimated that in the Lady Alice *he had sailed approximately* 1004 *miles in his circumnavigation of Lake Victoria.*

May 8th:

Halt at Kagehyi.

During my absence, three Chiefs conspired together to rob the Expedition, and for this purpose sought to induce Kaduma to join them, but Kaduma refused saying I was his stranger and absent and if they came to rob my goods they would have to fight him, which cooled them down, but Frank and Fred upon being informed of the conspiracy opened the ammunition cases and distributed 1500 rounds of ammunition to the men. Also the murderous Msenna endeavoured hard to induce the men to march with him to Unyanyembe. Many of the men listened to him and the 6th May was the day for the appearance of the new moon and for their departure. As it fortunately turned out, I arrived on the 5th May, the day before their plot was to take effect.

PART III

LAKE VICTORIA—LAKE TANGANYIKA

May 9th, 1875—July 31st, 1876

LAKE VICTORIA—LAKE TANGANYIKA

*Stanley halted in Kagehyi until May 29th, 1875. While re-
organising the Expedition, he had plenty to worry him. The 30
transport canoes promised by the King of Uganda did not arrive,
were reported to be still on the further side of brutal Bumbireh
Island, while the land route to westward was said to be impassable
for warring tribes and the savageries of the notorious Mirambo,
Chief of the Ruga-Ruga. A mission led by Frank Pocock to
Lukongeh, Sultan of Ukerewe, to procure the loan of canoes for a
water-journey to Uganda was despatched on May 16th. Stanley
suffered a sharp bout of fever, wrote reports to his sponsors, letters
to his friends, shot a boa-constrictor 11 feet long, overhauled the
ammunition and photographed Fred Barker's grave.*

May 29th:

Kagehyi.
Frank Pocock's and Prince Kaduma's mission to Lukongeh
King of Ukerewe was a failure. Whether it was their fault or
that of Lukongeh's I know not, but the spirit of the message
they were told to convey to Lukongeh was misconceived. The
canoes requested of the King were to carry the Expedition
along the western shore to Uganda, but Lukongeh sent them to
carry the Expedition to Ukerewe, a thing by no means desirable,
because its further progress might be endangered by the caprice
of the King. Therefore the 50 canoes with which Pocock returned were sent back, and I decided to accompany them to
endeavour to induce the King to yield to my wishes. Sailed
from Kagehyi at 8 a.m., and arrived at Kisorya at 4 p.m. in
Ukerewe across Speke Gulf.

May 31st:

Obtained an interview with the King, a handsome open-
faced light-coloured young man . . . The audience hall was the
open air, Lukongeh's throne was a rock. I discovered during
this interview that the King was as desirous of acquiring intelligence respecting Europe as Mtesa was, and that he was as
promising a subject for a convert to Christianity as the latter.

81

June 1st:

Had another interview with Lukongeh, at which after stating my errand I was promised as many canoes as I desired, but he requested me to be patient as his people were suspicious that I meant to take them to Uganda, but while he intended to induce them to believe that I intended to return to Ukerewe, between ourselves I was to receive them as if they were my own, and to do with the canoes as I wished.

Aware of the value of a reputation of Great Medicine-man, the King besought me earnestly several times to impart to him some of the secrets of Europe, such as medicine to make lions and leopards, to cause the rain-winds to come when called, to cause his women to be fruitful, and to give himself more virility. These demands are commonly made by the most ignorant and superstitious of African chiefs. When I stated my inability to comply with his wishes, he whispered aside to his Chiefs: "He will not give me what I ask, because he is afraid that he will not get the canoes, but you will see when my men return from Uganda, he will give me all I ask."

June 3rd:

Lukongeh announced to me privately yesterday afternoon that he would give me 30 canoes and two Wakerewe for each to accompany me to Uganda, for which I was to give him suitable gifts. If the Wakerewe were unable to bring the canoes back to him it did not matter, which was tidings most gratifying to me.

June 6th:

Halt at Msossi, Ukerewe.

The presents I am to give Lukongeh are 2 suits of English cloth [*of crimson and blue flannel*], medicine for rheumatism, headache, 1 revolver and ammunition, 1 bale of cloth, beads of various kinds, 1 cap, 1 English rug, one Kiganda canoe capable of carrying 40 men, 1 wife from Mtesa, 2 tusks of ivory, iron wire, and 1 coil of brass wire. All of which I have promised to give if possible. In return for which all canoes which accompany me to Usukuma from Ukerewe, I am to seize as my own, as well as the paddles. If the Wakerewe refuse to accompany me to Uganda, I am to permit them to depart for their own country how they may, but by no means surrender canoes or paddles.

Stanley bade farewell to King Lukongeh on June 7th and after some delay sailed back with a muster of 23 Wakerewe canoes across Speke Gulf to the waiting Expedition.

June 12th:

Arrived at Kagehyi with the canoes and in accordance with Lukongeh's instructions seized the canoes and paddles to the astonishment of the Wakerewe.

June 13th:

Today the Wakerewe to the number of 250 attempted to retake their canoes by force, but a few harmless shots dispersed them, and caused them to depart for Mwanza whence they purpose returning to Ukerewe. Two chiefs only in obedience to Lukongeh's whispered instructions accompany me to Uganda to receive Lukongeh's reward.

A halt for loading ensued and three-quarters of the Expedition, Uganda-bound, set sail on June 19th.

June 21st:

After a gale had subsided which lasted almost all the morning we sailed from Kunneneh Island, west towards Komeh Island. Though it was hard labour rowing against the heavy swell of the Lake, we got on tolerably well until sunset. Soon intense darkness set in, and I had recourse to lighting wax tapers to guide the canoes, in which were embarked 150 men, and all the property of the Expedition. By this means, and by threats of dreadful punishment for disobedience of orders, the canoes were kept together. We had proceeded quietly on for about two hours when suddenly shrill cries were heard as if from drowning men for "The Boat, the Boat".

Hurrying to the rescue I distinguished, to my astonishment, round things darker than the water apparently floating on it, which we soon found to be the heads of several men swimming away from a wrecked canoe. After taking these frightened people on board I asked where the property was that was in the canoe—4 bales of cloth, 1 case of ammunition, 2 bags of grain for provisions. "The bales float on the water, but the ammunition and grain have sunk with the canoe."

We hastily snatched up the bales, and distributed their cloth as well as we might among the largest of the canoes. We had scarcely moved from this scene, before we heard other shrill alarming cries for the boat. Another canoe was sinking, and while hastening towards the wreck I lit a wax taper, and set fire to the leaves of a book I had been reading during the afternoon, to light up the dread scene. Heads of struggling men and bales were found here likewise in the water, and a canoe turned bottom up, with a large rent in the side. Inquiring as to the result of the calamity, we heard to our alarm that five guns had sunk, and were lost, fortunately no beads, wire or ammunition. Again we distributed the men and cloth among the canoes, for the boat was up to her gunwales, with 17 men, and 30 loads on board, and if a breeze arose, unless we lightened her, she must inevitably sink.

Perceiving that if I persisted in my course for Komeh during the night I would endanger the Expedition greatly I changed it for Miandereh Islands a little south of west, and several miles nearer to us, and shouted into the darkness a threat that if any man lost his gun, he would be left to drown, and if any more canoes filled with water, they were to stay by them in the water until we could devise means to rescue them.

For a short time we proceeded on our way without further accident and the moon rose cheering our condition somewhat. But again cries broke out, and hurrying to the scene we found another canoe gunwales deep in water two men paddling vigorously, and five men engaged in baling her, and while we were endeavouring to plan how we could save them, another cry broke out, and a third one loudly called for assistance. In this extremity I scarcely knew not what to do [*sic*], all the sound canoes and boat were loaded, as far as safety permitted, and as a fourth cry alarmed me, I shouted out desperately: "You who would save yourselves follow me to the islands, and you who call for help do not leave your canoes, or let go your guns, float in the water laying hold of your canoes, until we return." Saying which, heedless of the piteous cries for help, we rowed hard and fast for Miandereh, which we reached within an hour.

Though it may seem to some unacquainted with our actual peril to have been a barbarous course to adopt, yet it was the only method available of saving the lives of more than half the Expedition, for if a breeze arose few would live in our over-loaded state to reach the islands of Miandereh. As soon as we reached the islands we unloaded four of the soundest canoes, and sent them back to render assistance, which arrived timely enough, for though three of the canoes sank, we saved all the men, goods and guns. Our losses during this fearful journey were five canoes, five guns, one case of ammunition, one bag of beads, and eight sacks of corn.

Arrived at Singo Island 8 miles West by North from Miandereh, half mile from Ito [*Island*].

The next morning left a third of the men, and goods, on the rocks of Miandereh, and proceeding to Singo Island not far off, disembarked property and some men, and sent them back to Miandereh for the remaining members of the Expedition, and on the 23rd halted to repair, the people beginning to learn after such cruel experience that their lives depended on the soundness of their canoes. At Kagehyi they were too indolent, though repeatedly warned to examine their canoes, and ignorant of their danger, made only the most superficial repairs.

June 24th:

On the 24th we arrived at Refuge Island altogether, having purchased 3 canoes at Ito Island, to replace the five wrecked.

June 25th:

I chose Refuge Island for the half-way station between Usukuma and Uganda, from its admirable means of defence, its quiet sunny coves, and its distance from the mainland which was sufficiently far to prevent invasion, and near enough to purchase provisions should it be necessary. On the island I halted one day to build a strong defensive camp, and to sur-round it with a fence of bush ten feet thick, which by rigorous measures was finished in one day. A stout house was also built to store the goods and grain for the subsistence of the garrison I intended to leave in it during my absence. Refuge Island was so named for the shelter given us in our distressed condition when we escaped from the hands of savage Bumbireh. It afforded a sufficiently extensive pasture area for our asses, and besides its advantages of quiet coves and isolation, its rocks formed a natural fortress which a few men with guns might make impregnable against such neighbours as Rusuvi and Uganda on the mainland, and I felt that I could depart from it with a feeling of perfect security as far as regarded the safety of its garrison.

June 26th:

After mustering the people, I collected 44 of the stoutest men as garrison under the command of Frank Pocock and Manwa Sera, and after seeing the property, which consisted of 36 bales of cloth, 17 cases of ammunition, 24 sacks of beads, 400 pounds of brass wire, and 12 loads of sundries, besides 60 sacks of grain, set sail with 21 canoes and 106 men for Usukuma to bring the remainder of the Expedition to our half-way station to Uganda . . .

Stanley sailed back to Kagehyi, arriving on June 30th.

July 4th:

[*Kagehyi.*]

. . . While down at the cove of Kagehyi superintending the repairing of a large canoe I purchased from Kipingiri, Prince Kaduma's brother, one of my people came running to me crying out that my people were drunk and killing one another. Running up to discover why the riot was permitted by the Captain in charge, I saw one of my men dead lying by a hut with a deep gash in his throat, another staggering along with a spear cut on his head, and a third with a bludgeon blow on the temple, marking the ground with blood, and while gazing astounded at this scene, a drunken infuriate came rushing up to me, and aimed a smarting blow at my head with a bloody bludgeon. Fortunately springing aside I avoided the blow, and pinioned his arms, calling for a cord with which when procured we bound him hand and foot. Another was treated in the same manner, and finally ascertaining who the murderer of the dead man was, bound him, and clapped the three in chains until matters could be inquired into . . .

July 5th:

After an inquiry by which the cause of the riot was ascertained, the murderer of Membé, one of my stout boat-bearers, Fundi Rehani, was sentenced to 200 lashes and to be kept in chains until he could be delivered up to the proper authorities; the two drunkards to 100 lashes each, and to be kept in chains for 6 months . . .

Stanley embarked the rear echelon of the Expedition and sailed from Kagehyi on July 6th, arriving at Refuge Island on July 11th. The re-united Expedition halted there for 7 nights.

July 17th:

Refuge Island. Halt.

The constant anxiety induced by the peril of the Expedition while travelling on the Lake, and the vast amount of care and solicitude lavished on the journey, quite knocked me up by the day I arrived at Refuge Island, so that for six days I was so ill that I was confined to bed, and on the sixth day when able to rise I was so weak that I was unable to roam over the quiet friendly island which had formerly been our Refuge in distress, and had now been the sole asylum of a large number of the Expedition for nearly a month.

But the men had not been idle, they knew every nook and cranny of it, they had also got attached to their island home. About 15 fruit trees were found on the eastern side, loaded with delicious fruit the size of a cherry. The stones are two in number, like small date stones. The flavour of it had something between a custard apple, and a ripe gooseberry. The garrison failed to consume a half of the quantity of the sweet fruit, so that arriving with about 150 more people there was sufficient left for them to remember the sweet fruit of Refuge Island. The leaf of the tree is like a peach tree leaf, and the fruit generally hangs in threes. The wood is tough and flexible [*probably a species of the Verbenaceae*]. Kijaju King of Komeh furnished us with a guide to take as far as Uganda. His assistance was valuable only in giving me the names of localities.

July 18th:

Arrived at Kazaradzi Island. Our guide propitiated the Victoria with a green banana leaf, saying "Be kind to us, O

Nyanza. Give the White M'kama a safe and prosperous passage."

The setting of the sun witnessed from Kazaradzi Island was grand in the extreme. The sun descending beyond the horizon and leaving the clouds behind him transformed them into gold. The sky seemed as if melted gold had been thrown hot against it, when it had suddenly cooled and become fixed, or like a picture against which a sponge immersed in gold colour had been dashed, for the cloudlets far on the right and on the left of the west, resembled great splotches, and even halfway up the zenith might be seen the same spots.

They sailed on, arriving at Mahyiga Island on July 21st, where they heard news of their dilatory Waganda escort and prepared to punish the malignant population of Bumbireh Island.

July 22nd:

Halt at Mahyiga Island.

The afternoon of the day the canoes of the Expedition appeared at Mahyiga Island, two large canoes came from Iroba towards the cove on the beach of which our canoes were drawn up. On hailing us, they received a friendly answer, and in return gave us the long desired information respecting Magassa the Grand Admiral of Mtesa. It appeared that Magassa arrived and camped on Mahyiga Island—as we had suspected from the abandoned camps we discovered thereon—four days after we had escaped from Bumbireh; that Magassa was told that our oars and drum had been taken from us, upon which the two Wangwana left with Magassa as a guard of honour, declared that we were murdered as the oars were our "feet" without which we could not move. "There is no doubt of it" said the Wangwana, "for how could they have taken the oars without fighting for them, and what could a few men do against a large island like Bumbireh." The people of Iroba and Bumbireh assured the angry men repeatedly that the white man had escaped after killing 14 people. Magassa advised that they should proceed south for two or three days, in the hope of obtaining news, but the Wangwana declared persistently against such a proceeding, and councilled a return to Mtesa to ask for revenge.

After staying two days the foolish Magassa demanded the oars and drum, and then returned conveying them to Mtesa with the intelligence that we were murdered. Upon which the King sent messengers to Kytawa and Antari, Kings of Uzongora and Ihangiro, commanding them to search for the white man, and not to abstain from the search until they had found certain tidings of him.

[*We*] having no means at hand to verify this news, the natives of Iroba were informed that we had come for the oars and the drum, and must not be refused, otherwise I would attack their island, and destroy them, to which they replied that the Kings of Bumbireh and Ihangiro should be informed of my message.

The afternoon of the next day the two Kings sent word that Magassa had truly taken the oars and drum to Uganda, and Antari of Ihangiro had commanded his subject King of Bumbireh to furnish us with provision, and the natives of Iroba declared that if we did them no harm they would bring us abundance of food.

I waited for this food until 4 p.m. of the 23rd, and perceiving, or at least suspecting that they were trifling with me, I manned ten canoes and the boat, and proceeded to Iroba to enforce what they had promised. As we made our appearance the natives hurried to the beach with the bullocks, and food. They were told that it was a bad thing to trifle with men they had attempted to kill and had robbed, and that they had best convey the bullocks and the food to our camp. On [*their*] promising strict obedience, we left the shore, and rowed hard to Bumbireh, and about sunset appeared off Kajurri, before the natives of whom we manoeuvred to shew that we had really returned, and that they must expect war if our demands were not complied with. Then returning to camp on Mahyiga Island we arrived in time to meet the natives of Iroba, with the supplies.

On surveying this party, I discovered that two persons in it were of such importance that by detaining them, I possibly might be able to obtain what I wanted without hostilities which if commenced would undoubtedly cause the innocent to suffer with the guilty. For I had resolved upon having the person of the treacherous King of Bumbireh, and two of his principal Chiefs in my power, and after preaching to them about their wickedness and folly, to return them safe to Bumbireh to shew that the White man was, although strong, very kind hearted. Accordingly the two Chiefs which brought the provisions were told they must stop on the island, quietly if they would, in chains if they would not, until Shekka King of Bumbireh, and two of his Chiefs were in my hands. One of these I detained was the Chief of the island of Iroba, the other was the son of a Chief of Ihangiro. They were startled at this information, but I gave them no time to make resistance and the detention was peaceable enough. Finding himself a prisoner, the Chief of Iroba communicated instructions to his men how to capture the King of Bumbireh, and his two sub-chiefs. As they were about to move off, two others were seized in order to ensure the utmost effort of their friends to effect what I wished.

This plan was partially successful, for on the afternoon of the 24th the men of Iroba brought Shekka to me with all the clothes and beads he had received of me, but the two sub-chiefs were not found. In return for this service, I released the Chief of Iroba, and one of his men.

As the Chief of Iroba was about to leave our island camp in his canoe, I informed him that I would certainly keep the Chief of Ihangiro's son if the principal actors in the villainy enacted at Bumbireh were not placed in my hands. The King of Bumbireh was put in chains to avoid worse treatment by the boat's crew who remembered his wicked treacherous face too well. To obtain his release he promised all his cattle, sheep, goats, wives and children, his fears of capital punishment were so terrible. As he prayed for his life, which indeed was never my intention to take, he was as cunningly pitiful, as his former ferocity, and thirst for our blood made him hideously villainous.

About midnight two of the prisoners that were free on parole attempted to escape, one was caught in the act, the other was not taken until the middle of the next day and then was found at the entrance of a small cave making signals to a canoe approaching from Iroba. For this act the prisoners were all chained.

July 26th:

Halt on Mahyiga Island.
Now that I had become interested in these incidents, it was

not possible for me to leave Mahyiga Island to return for the garrison and cattle left on Refuge Island. I therefore sent Manwa Sera with the canoes, lest in my absence more mischief might be wrought by the treacherous natives of Bumbireh. I also heard news from Iroba that some Waganda were on the mainland, which was another inducement for me to remain, as I expected they might be searching parties sent by Mtesa.

July 27th:

Halt on Mahyiga Island.

Two Waganda messengers made their appearance in a large canoe manned by 40 men, who said they were sent by Sabadu, a chief of Mtesa, in charge of ten canoes bound to Ukerewe, and a little after this arrival another Kiganda canoe came up from the mainland with salaams from Mkwanga, another chief of Uganda, sent by Mtesa to hunt up news of his white stranger, which considering our want of transport, and the rotten state of our canoes, was most welcome news. An abundance of ripe bananas, gourds full of Uganda wine, and a few goats presented to us made them still more welcome. Mkwanga had searched the lands of Mtatembwa, Kytawa, Kamiru and Ihangiro in vain for news of me, when just as he was about to give up the search rumour reached of our arrival with a "large fleet" of canoes near Bumbireh, to which island he despatched his men to certify his news.

July 28th:

Halt on Mahyiga Island.

Six large Kiganda canoes appeared from another quarter, namely Alice Island, whither they had gone to search for me, and where they heard of my arrival at Bumbireh. The timely arrival of these several parties at our island camp made the prospect more encouraging, for by virtue of my influence with Mtesa, I was bold enough to detain Sabadu for my service, that his canoes might carry the remainder of the men, cattle and asses to Uganda, by which means we would have to make but one journey of it. Meantime I disguised the fact of having sent back the canoes to Refuge Island from the natives of Bumbireh by not permitting their canoes to land at the southern cove, before which our camp was built, and confined myself only to verbal demands for the two Sub-chiefs of Bumbireh Island.

July 29th:

Halt on Mahyiga Island.

Eight more canoes belonging to Mtesa made their appearance, and as Sabadu and Mkwanga placed themselves at my orders, I was furnished with quite an imposing force. Our 21 canoes, and the 16 Kiganda canoes, made the number 37 capable of carrying 548 men for such was now the actual number of the Anglo-American Expedition united with the Waganda. The Kiganda canoes were manned by 480 men, several of them having 40 paddlers. As the coves of Mahyiga Island were not large enough to enable all our canoe fleet to be beached I sent the Waganda to Iroba, where for a few days at least they could also obtain sufficient subsistence.

July 30th:

Halt on Mahyiga Island.

Suspecting from the long delay that the two Chiefs of Bumbireh refused to be entrapped, and not desirous of pushing the natives to extremities, I sent to Antari of Ihangiro, who in reality was the Lord of these isles, that if he would redeem my prisoners including the King of Bumbireh, I would accept 5 bullocks, 30 bill-hooks and 40 spears, and proclaim peace, and gave him 3 days to reflect on it. The alternative was that I would punish the natives of Bumbireh, and take all my prisoners with [*me*] to Mtesa King of Uganda, to be dealt with by him, whose subject he was, as he only saw fit.

Three clear days elapsed. Antari did not condescend to reply.

August 3rd:

Halt on Mahyiga Island.

. . . Manwa Sera returned from Refuge Island with the remnant of the Expedition, men, cattle, asses, all safe, though the latter were considerably bruised from the effects of the cords which bound them. It now only remained to settle matters with Antari and proceed on our voyage to Uganda, happy that all difficulties had been overcome. But Antari was not disposed to yield tamely to a demand of any kind from the white man, for I learned that he had been despatching men and canoes to assist Bumbireh, and this morning I received a most insolent message from him to the effect that if I did not surrender my prisoners he would attack me. To prove this spirit I despatched ten canoes of the Waganda to Bumbireh for provisions, and the result was that they [*the Waganda*] were defeated, one was killed and 8 wounded, and the Waganda reported that Bumbireh was full of men from Ihangiro, and as they got into their canoe the natives shouted that they would see certain mischief the next day. That night I called Sabadu and Mkwanga from Iroba with all their canoes and men, and shewed them a plan of attack by the Wangwana alone by which none of our party would be injured and none of the Waganda engaged except as passive spectators, which met of course their approval.

August 4*th:*

Halt on Mahyiga Island.

A strong gale lasted all the morning but at noon it moderated, and I embarked 250 men in 6 large canoes and the boat, and proceeded towards Bumbireh Island. We did not molest Iroba as that island had already done noble penance, and as we had become stout friends with them, we passed it with a cheery salutation to its natives lining the shore. After two hours hard pulling we arrived close to Bumbireh, the hated island, the savage ferocity of whose people I have seldom seen equalled.

As we approached its south-western extremity I signalled the canoes to close up, and steered the boat which was in the advance towards a small cove, as if with the purpose of dis-embarking at that spot. Having seen us approach so close as to admit of no doubt but that we intended to land, the scouts on the headlands who had until then remained motionless, sounded the alarm and disappeared behind a banana plantation. But instead of landing, I rounded the cove, and steering close to the land under the lee of the isle we pulled hard, and after half an hour entered a noble bay on the western side of the Island and behind Kajurri. This was a manoeuvre, which despite their natural foxy astucity the natives had not counted on, nor were they aware until they had paid a most fatal debt how completely they had placed themselves in my power. Had I landed at the little cove at the south-west I should have had to breast a steep hill with over a thousand spears, arrows, and rocks flying from under cover of a leafy plantation of bananas, but by entering this bay I could land where I pleased if I wished and choose my own position, but I did not intend to land, for I should then assuredly have injured myself, a thing by no means to be desired, when the fighting men are also the transport force of an Expedition. What I intended, and had planned to do was to pull steadily and slowly in one direction, and so draw the natives to that point—which should be clear and open ground—in a body to contest the supposed disembarkation, and then pour volley after volley upon them until they confessed themselves amply punished. I also had planned to attack them at a point where the sun would be an ally in my favour, for as it declines to the west, it has a powerfully dazzling and blinding effect in the tropics, when it naturally is hottest.

With these views I formed a regular line of battle at the entrance of the bay and conveyed my instructions to the riflemen, which were to wait coolly until they were within a short distance from the shore, and then to take deliberate aim but by no means to land, as I wanted none of my own punished, but to punish Bumbireh, with the power of a father punishing a stubborn and disobedient son. After this warning I gave the word to push on, and in an orderly and deliberate manner, we advanced upon a shore which rose almost immediately from the water's edge, and formed a steep hill, covered with short grass, and utterly devoid of even the slightest bush or twig. To this point as I had imagined the natives rose in a body from their covert, and rushed to defend, with the idea no doubt that it offered as good advantages to them as the place they had selected if we landed there, as indeed it would have done. We allowed them to mass themselves as they wished, and, after we had approached within fifty yards, I waited awhile to give the soldiers time to take aim, and at the word we poured a volley into them with tolerable good effect, for which in return we received a copious shower of rocks, and arrows, which fell harmlessly in the water.

After the first volley, each man fired his rifle deliberately and to each shot a yell of defiance was uttered, and either a rock or an arrow was sent with desperate effort in return. Our line was soon broken, as the men warmed to their work, and each soldier compelled his paddlers to approach nearer, where their aim would be more fatal, for which temerity some of them received bloody crowns, but it soon was evident that the method was more effective, by the rapid thinning of the savages, by the numbers of dead which strewed the hill slope, and the wounded who were seen painfully limping, or crawling up, passing the gauntlet of showers of bullets, on their weary way. The Savages were not a whit disheartened. Relief after relief came gallantly down, and with a frenzied courage stood the brunt. Several of the boldest even advanced into the water and seemed to shoot their arrows in scorn, but these were soon seen gasping in the water, and a few gurgles only marked where they stood. After an hour and a half, the decline of their courage, and cooling of their ferocity all their bluster and shouting could not conceal. The water's edge became clear, and a more respectable distance was maintained, and as the soldiers became conscious of their success, these last were also conquered, until now Waganda and Wangwana joined in a clamorous request to be permitted to land, and decapitate the dead. But this was peremptorily refused, and after shouting through an interpreter, that the white man had punished them in a manner they would remember and warned them in future to leave strangers alone, I ordered the bugle to sound the return. We reached camp after sunset without incident, the Wangwana and Waganda immeasurably elated at our success.

On reckoning up the results of our hostile intercourse with Bumbireh, we had great cause to feel gratified. We had the King of Bumbireh and one of his subjects, besides a chief, and a chief's son of Ihangiro in our power, chained at our mercy. In the attack, the natives lost 33 killed on the spot, and probably over a hundred wounded, many no doubt fatally, while during our successful escape some two months before they had lost 14 killed, from which great losses the savages no doubt will learn in future to behave with some regard to the rights of strangers. It had been a common practice with them to seize on all canoes, Waganda or Wakerewe, and hold their crews as slaves; such could not have been our fate as we were too well armed to be captured so tamely, but had we not been successful in our escape, this exact story of our adventures had not been written.

The next day at dawn we embarked in our canoes and proceeded in a body along the shores of Iroba and Bumbireh, to the former waving friendly farewells, to the latter with angry rifles, one of which had fatal effect at over a thousand yards distance. The natives of Bumbireh for the first time saw the full power against which they were opposed and felt great trepidation at the sight, and retreated in detached bodies to the summit of the highest hills, which was very different from their behaviour the day before. Had we stayed one day longer, we should have received tribute, and professions of peace. Old Shekka the King viewed his island as he passed it with sad, regretful eyes, and at the sight I felt more than half inclined to land him on the shore, and then and there forgive him. Had he shed one tear I should have done so, or had he asked me, but the captive King though sad-looking was mute and tearless.

We made a brave show as we proceeded along the coast, the canoes 37 in number containing 500 men paddling to the sound of sonorous drums, and the cheery tones of the bugle, the English, American and Zanzibar flags flying gaily in unison with a most animating scene. To test the effect of yesterday's battle on the spirit of the natives, we made a point of landing at the north-western extremity of the island, when we were hailed by a group, and told to "go in peace." "Enough, enough," said they. "We have done!" Which we took to be a confession that their bluster for the time had been utterly vanquished, and accordingly continued on our way, and at night beached our canoes on the shore of Ukara, in Uzongora, King Kamiru's country.

The next day we were beset with congratulations, and gifts from the Kings Kytawa and Kamiru. Three oxen, three goats, and 50 bunches of bananas, besides milk, chickens, and ripe plantains in abundance. Kytawa, requested by his neighbour Antari of Ihangiro, commenced negotiations for the redemption of the captives. I consented to release them on payment of an indemnity of 50 bill-hooks and 40 spears, provided that they should be furnished me within ten days. Kytawa also received a message from Bumbireh stating that the white man was destroying them, and the news that two villages lost 17 killed

H. M. Stanley after the 1874 expedition.

Photograph : Walery

Edward and Frank Pocock and the *Lady Alice*.
From the Illustrated London News

in the fight. Kytawa refused to interfere, sternly saying to them: "You have not suffered half enough for what cause had you to molest the White man. Besides you have slain one of my chiefs and wounded two more. Away with you, and look out for me next."

After a day's halt at friendly Ukara, we sailed to Musira Island, having had good cause to call Kytawa and Kamiru friendly, as besides provisions they sent eight canoes to assist us as far as Uganda, which increased the number of our transport force to 45. Arrived at Musira Island, the inhabitants of Makongo dreading punishment for their unfriendliness on a former occasion sent us of their own free will two bullocks, five goats, and one hundred bunches of bananas, in return for which their Chief received presents of cloth, as a token of peace. Brutal Kyozza, King of Northern Uzongora, also sent a most friendly message to the effect that he hoped we would visit his shores, as he had ten oxen to give me. The Waganda chiefs implored me not to accept his gifts, as he was an enemy of Mtesa, whom one day he [*Mtesa*] intended to destroy for horribly mutilating ten of his messengers and detaining on several occasions the tribute due to him, as lord of his country. Having no cause for hostilities with Kyozza, I compromised the matter, and in return for his friendly request, I declined civilly, saying that I was in a hurry to reach Uganda.

Thus was our victory at Bumbireh productive of great good and plenty to us. The fame of it was already widely spread along the shores of the mainland, for though these natives do not possess the means of Europe and America to communicate news, yet rumour is swift and industrious.

The victorious Expedition sailed on towards the metropolitan territories of King Mtesa.

August 12th:

From Mezinda, we sailed to Dumo, Uganda, which from its position nearly half way between the Katonga and the Kagera [*Rivers*] I selected as a camp where the Expedition could rest from its perilous and long voyage while I proceeded to Mtesa to obtain guides for the overland journey to the Albert Nyanza.

The Lake Albert to which Stanly henceforth refers was in fact the body of water now known as Lake Edward. The geography of this part of Africa was still to be accurately established, and largely through Stanley's own efforts.

Having landed I proceeded to select a suitable and healthy locality, and chose the high ground below the cove of Dumo whence we had a fine view of the bay of Isangu, to the south and to the east, as far as Sesse. On this spot the camp was arranged in the form of a broad street fronted at either end by the respective houses of the Commander and the Father of the Expedition. The canoes of Ukerewe were beached and condemned, the houses were built in an orderly and symmetrical manner, the flag posts were raised, and having arranged for provisions during my absence, and given instructions to Frank Pocock, and the Father for the government of the camp, I set sail in the boat, accompanied by the canoes of the Waganda to visit Mtesa.

Stimulated by the rumours of war between Mtesa and his vassals, and lamenting the death of Jack, his bull-terrier, gored by a wild cow, Stanley hastened towards the Ripon Falls where the royal forces were assembled.

August 19th:

Halt at Ntewi.

Received a fat bullock and an abundance of milk. Messenger sent with my ring, given me by Sir John Bennett of London, from Mahyiga Island, returned with kind greetings from the Kabaka and his Chiefs and an invitation to hurry up to him before he went to war with Uvuma.

Chowpereh and Muccadum also came to me and declared the true cause of our misfortunes at Bumbireh to be the dilatoriness of Magassa the Grand Admiral, who seems to have been nearly beheaded for his vanity and dilatoriness.

We carried the boat a quarter of a mile inland and built a house over it that it may be safe from the prying eyes of the Wavuma rovers, who appear to understand the art of naval warfare on the Lake to perfection: I hear of them advancing upon Mtesa with 300 canoes! They fight desperately and are expert divers, attack their enemy in the open lake, dive under the canoes and cut the vegetable cords which fasten the boat.

The oars stolen from Stanley at Bumbireh were in the safe keeping of the Chief of Ntewi. Stanley recovered them when he returned to Ntewi in mid-November.

August 23rd:

Arrived at Jinja, Usoga, on the eastern side of the Ripon Falls, at the camp of the King. Was received with joy and honour by King and chiefs.

August 24th:

Today I was received in state by Mtesa, such state as is not to be found in Africa out of Egypt. Thousands of men in line, hundreds of soldiers bearing guns. Chiefs to the number of a hundred and more, Mtesa sitting regally on a large chair covered with cloth of gold. He has promised me a small army to open the region lying between Uganda and Albert Nyanza [*L. Edward*], with which I hope to overcome every obstacle. He is ever anxious to please white men and to open commerce between Uganda and Europe.

August 26th:

Nambija a young Mganda who had the misfortune to share my misfortunes on the Lake after the wicked Magassa had deserted his trust, had the ill luck to play with one of my revolvers in the Court of Mtesa and to fire one shot, which came near the loss of his head, had I not begged his life. The Wakungu [*senior army officers*] are frequently beheaded; given to the charge of Kasaju who is the executioner; no news is heard of them again. When Katekiro—the Prime Minister— otherwise called Pokino asked me for medicine which caused death to be painless, I wondered; but when I heard such news I no longer wondered. Mtesa proposes to march tomorrow to Magongo, the camp of Sekibobo.

August 27th:

This morning Mtesa's army consisting of some 150 thousand warriors marched, accompanied with something like 50,000 women, and 50,000 slaves and boys. Mtesa's face was covered with a whitish paste, his head was uncovered and he wore a blue check dress. Katekiro marched before the King in a black coat, while Mtesa followed him surrounded by his soldiers. About 2,000 spearmen—shields—preceded him on the trot and as Chief after Chief followed hard after with their hundreds and thousands, it seemed that the doom of Uvuma had been written. Besides this, over 400 large canoes, containing upwards of 20 men each, under the charge of Kautu, carrying say 10,000 men, followed the shore line. Old Sawagansi, the King's first wife's mother [*father*] had an army of about 400 women, besides about 1,000 spearmen. He had also brought his pointers with him like an English Squire for he loves dogs greatly. After our departure 200 canoes of the Wavuma approached the deserted camp and set fire to it besides killing some dozen sick people that were left there . . .

The royal army and fleet took up positions to prosecute the war against the Wavuma defending the island of Ingira.

August 30th:

We are within sight and hearing of the Wavuma. I suppose they have about 300 canoes. They are very boastful and exhibit mad antics to us.

September 1st:

The Waganda under Sekibobo occupying Magongo launched their canoes and struck across the Bay to this camp. The Wavuma attacked them, captured 5 canoes; the remainder, 190 in number, arrived safely amid shouts of welcome from the entire army. A little later we cannonaded the island of Ingira, doing some damage to canoes and killing a few men.

September 2nd:

This day has been idle. Mtesa's army is immense and over-powering, but his fleet is vastly inferior to the Wavuma, while the enemy musters nearly 300 large and small canoes and some 6,000 expert sailors. He has but 190 canoes and but 3,000 sailors . . .

September 6th:

Halt [*at Nakaranga*].
Began a causeway yesterday of trees and brush to connect the headland of Nakaranga with Ingira. By tonight we have taken

50 yards out of the 700 of water that separate the two points. The Lake begins to belch forth the dead in the late passage of the bay. I have begun to translate the Scriptures for Mtesa in the intervals of war business. A cannon I aimed at the island has caused 5 deaths. Today I dropped two with a Snyder rifle. As I have embraced Mtesa's offer to see him, I am in as much danger as he or any of his men is, if I meet the Wavuma. It therefore behoves me to exert my skill to get the Waganda victory.

September 9th:

Against my advice Mtesa sent a peace party under a favourite boy soldier of his named Wibba in a canoe. We watched the canoe until it touched the shore, and then it became engulphed in a mad crowd of black demons who slaughtered them to a man before our eyes and laughed the King to scorn.

Mtesa spoke today of building a large boat, or a small schooner.

September 10th:

Halt.

The causeway is progressing, Scripture is being translated, and we touch now and then upon the wonders of nature, the Heavens, the air, nature of rocks etc., all of which is hailed with wonder by the Sultan and his people.

The Sultan of Usogu arrived yesterday with a thousand magnificent looking creatures of a most warlike appearance, plumes, wavy hair of monkeys, spears, feathers, shields and wild strange music. Some of them wore the oddest and most fantastic head-dresses I have yet seen, such as young kids stuffed, young leopards and young lions, braves in leopard skins and lions' manes.

September 12th:

Halt.

It is proposed to fight tomorrow, though the causeway is but advanced 70 yards out of the 700.

September 13th:

At day-break 40 canoes were manned with infantry— musketeers—and sallied out to give the Wavuma battle. They

101

formed line between Nakaranga Point and Ingira. Four cannons and 50 muskets were planted on the wooden causeway. The Wavuma formed 3 divisions of 60 canoes each, while the opposing heights were lined with thousands of spectators. At a signal from their Chiefs, the Wavuma came dashing like racers and yelling shrilly. It was one of the most exciting sights I ever witnessed. They were allowed to come within short musket distance. Then the Waganda line began to move slowly towards the shore firing their guns, disclosing the causeway with its murderous ambush. Finding the firing too hot for them the Wavuma sullenly retreated.

September 14th:

Halt.
Today I planned a new mode of fighting the Wavuma, placed 3 canoes together and built a palisade round the outer ones to conceal the rowers, who consist of timid paddlers from Sesse Island near Katonga river.

September 16th:

The floating fort two storeys high planned the day before yesterday was launched and tried to the unbounded admiration of Mtesa and his army and the visible surprise of the Wavuma on Ingira heights.

> "The invention all admired and each how he
> To be the Inventor missed, so easy it seemed
> Once found, which yet unfound most would have thought
> Impossible."
>
> Milton. I. 499

September 17th:

Halt.
Mtesa proposes to return. I object to it, and advise him to fight for his honour, which would be laughed at.

September 18th:

Halt.
A battle of canoes as before. The fort is not engaged because none of the enemy's canoes will come near it. Waganda punished well the Wavuma; they were as cool and collected

as veterans, for fear of Mtesa who had threatened to burn the cowards at the stake.

September 21st:

Another naval battle was fought today to the decided advantage of the Waganda. The Waganda improve daily—178 Wavuma canoes fought today against 122 Waganda, though there were about 80 Waganda canoes unengaged. Notwithstanding, the Wavuma deserve the praise for bravery and intrepidity. They show abundant proofs of a high courage while the Waganda displayed today at least coolness and skill. Neither party lost a canoe but the Wavuma lost heavily in men. If the Waganda possessed courage and a little dash they might have captured several Wavuma canoes. The floating fort has not yet been engaged because no one is found bold enough to take it to the battle, because with it they cannot run away. They must either fight or die.

September 22nd:

Another fight today between 214 Waganda canoes against 203 Wavuma canoes. The Wavuma after a couple of hours' inactivity advanced in a straight line, firm and compact like tigers, and brushed the Waganda away from the skirts of their island as if they were so many flies, and almost captured several of them. Mtesa is like a child. It is useless to advise him; any of his slaves or chiefs who will flatter him makes him oblivious of all counsel tending to his honour. The Wavuma deserve all praise for their hardihood and courage, while the Waganda to me make themselves objects of contempt. The Waganda have broken the *boma* because it would not [*let them*] run away fast enough. Mtesa has asked me today for the second time to give him my ammunition, and I have refused him, because I should be as one committing self-murder. Hence I consider it doubtful that he will give me men to guide me to Muta Nzige [*L. Edward*].

September 23rd:

Halt.
I hear he intends that I shall build his boat at Usavara though I have come so far to assist him with my advice and

powder against his enemies. He takes not this into consideration nor the valuable presents I have given him. I have written well of him, but I begin to think I was too premature in my praise, and that I shall have to bitterly lament that I returned to Uganda.

The war dragged on and the Wavuma did not put out peace feelers until October 6th. Stanley spent his time in religious conferences with Mtesa, and in elaborating his notes with full length essays on Waganda military organization, medicine, language, etc.

October 8th:

Halt.

The Sultan [*Mtesa*] asked his chiefs today which book they would accept to guide them in their duty to God. The Chiefs with one accord said, "We will take the White Man's Bible." Sultan said he would also, as he could not understand the Mohammedan book. Wavuma say they will come tomorrow to make peace.

October 12th:

Halt.

. . . Sultan told me today that he renounced Mohammedanism and became a Christian.

October 14th:

Halt.

The Wavuma brought two young girls as tribute and the war is over. The canoes 225 in number were ordered at once off and the Wavuma set up a glad shout. Later ten came to the Sultan. It is said we shall leave tomorrow.

October 15th:

We set out from Nakaranga after the war was over about 3 a.m. Few knew we should start. The first certainty we had when the huge Jojussu or big drum sounded the march. Then all began to pack up, but I was hardly dressed before my people shouted out to me that the entire camp was fired. I had just time to say Heavens! when I told the Wangwana to snatch up everything, and move after me. The roads though 100 feet wide were impassable owing to the fierce leaping waves of flame that rolled over the roads. There was only one way left and that was run before the flames up the mountain of Nakaranga, and thus make a wide detour. We were not alone in our attempt to realise the idea. There were at least 600,000 human beings struggling in a solid body in the same direction, trampling down the weak, aged and sick in their devouring haste to be away from the sea of fire below. It was a grand scene but a cruel one—for hundreds of sick, little ones and witless men and women perished in it. The flames almost took my breath away, they seemed to lick the air before it entered my lungs, but with heads bent low we charged on blindly, knowing no guide saving self interest and self preservation. I kept my people together by dint of severity, as several were more than half inclined to give up. We had an hour of such work for the camp was 3 miles long, and then a hard day's march until 3 p.m. which took us considerably more than half way to Jinja. By 7 p.m. I had the entire satisfaction to see my people all about me, separate, in a well selected camp, thankful that we were out of that heedless, reckless rush of human beings.

October 23rd:

Halt at Chikakanya.

Sent a letter to Frank at Dumo by one of Mtesa's messengers asking him to send me a prayer book to teach Mtesa Christian prayers.

Stanley marched with Mtesa to Ulagalla, the old capital of the Empire. Rubaga, the new capital, was about a mile and a half to the south of it.

November 6th:

Halt [*at Ulagalla*].

Recovered from a fit of two days' severe illness. Bull, my bulldog, had a severe attack of fever at the same time but he has recovered today after 3 days. The medicine I gave him was castor oil, $\frac{1}{2}$ ounce, and new milk, but he starved the fever out. The church foundations were laid on the summit of a hill adjoining the Palace. Thus Mtesa begins his new faith with ardor. Another church will be built at Rubaga, which will be the Cathedral. I also made Mtesa a fancy hammock or a *dhooly*, I forget what they call it in India, where coolies carry officers from place to place.

November 7th:

Frightful thunder claps. Built a church model for Mtesa.

November 8th:

Mtesa is the most intelligent African, who owes his intelligence to his own natural capacity, in or out of Africa I ever saw. His faculties are of a very high order. He is not adverse to flattery, and herein is one weak fault, he is also too fond of women, he is very courteous to ladies of the Royal Family, descendants of Kamanya and Suna [*former kings*], embraces them, speaks smilingly, bows, pays affable attention when they speak, though he does not stoop, as our super-European Royalties do, to do humble service to ladies. Indeed it will be many a hundred years yet before kings of Uganda will have acquired that proud art.

When he blows his nose, the three greatest Chiefs rush down on their knees, and implore the honour of brushing or drying the mucus from the napkin.

If he smiles, the whole Court smiles. If he frowns, instantly all wear submissive patient looks. If he storms, all fall prone to the ground, and swear to clutch the moon for him should he desire.

Often have they caught full grown lions, leopards, crocodiles, boa constrictors alive for him.

November 9th:

Within the Palace Courts.

Nine Courts to go through. Tenth, the Royal Burzah, is where levees are held each morning. Behind the public burzah is a smaller one, where the Chiefs—a few of the principal— meet with the King in the afternoons. The preceding Courts are mostly crowded with the people of the King's household, pages, soldiers, peasants, butchers, food providers, executioners, officers of the gates and courts, all mixed socially when not on duty. White dresses mingle with the clay colour of the native cloth robes.

Each Court is fenced round with tall cane fences neatly lashed together, and trees with beautiful green leaves line the fences. At each gate stand the guards opposing and giving egress and ingress. The household women of the King are beyond the tenth Court and have their separate Courts, according to their rank. The King's house contains a vast variety of rich dresses, curios and gifts from white people and Arabs. His bedstead is of iron, with a rich crimson carpet.

People of the guards have their food cooked and brought to them from the inner courts, beef and cooked bananas—and each order have their several allowances which are as liberal as they can desire given to them. After finishing, they all kneel and give thanks to the King in a loud voice with folded hands . . .

With the permission and military support of King Mtesa Stanley left the capital on November 13th to return to the Expedition still in camp at Dumo. He rejoined his men on November 20th after an absence of 3 months and 5 days. He then set about preparations for marching to Lake Edward.

November 24th:
_____

Halt at Dumo.

I prepared cartridges for the road. One clever fellow having seen Zazinie a dog from the Coast and my Jack and Bull, and having seen Speke, Grant and other Europeans, Long Bey, self, and Abdul Azziz Bey, asked: "Why is it that you Whites have all long noses and your dogs short noses, while we have short noses and our dogs have long noses?"

November 25th:
_____

. . . Tomorrow, being all ready, I propose to move once more towards the Albert Nyanza or Muta Nzige. [*L. Edward.*]

The Expedition set out on November 26th relying on Mtesa's promise of a military escort under the generalship of Sambuzi, a distinguished soldier, to lead them at least to the frontier of the Empire. But the Expedition had marched 86 miles through doubtful country, Stanley all the while worrying lest Mtesa should have reneged on his royal word, before it made contact with its escort on December 22nd.

107

December 23rd:

Met at last at Laugurwe the dilatory Sambuzi. I call him dilatory because he has been so laggard; he may improve, however, on the way.

December 24th:

Halt.

I have decided to listen to Mtesa's request and Dallington's desire, and permit the boy Dallington to return to Mtesa to teach him English and to confirm him in the faith which he has adopted. It may be better in the end for all concerned and for all European travellers in Uganda. I regret much indeed to part with the boy for he was a faithful, good and honest lad, a credit to the labours of the English Mission at Zanzibar.

December 25th:

Marched to Kibanda's village, a Mtongoloh of Kimbugwe. 6 miles West by North.

Look where I may, I see but hollow slopes and ridges, hardly a square mile level, the valleys along which we travel are generally long but narrow, and all drain into the Katonga. The prospect is bounded to all points with lines of blue hills, between a rolling open country scantily dotted with ant hills overgrown with long grass and brush and the *euphorbia* which seems to be the only tree above ground in all this region. One of the Waganda was speared in the hip today by natives who are affronted by our appearance. Our present strength may be estimated thus

Anglo/American Expedition	180 souls
Sambuzi (General)	1,000
Mkoma (Colonel)	250
Kurji (Captain)	40
Ngezi (Colonel)	250
Sekajugu (Colonel)	450
Mrowla (Colonel)	100
	2,270

With the expectation of reinforcement by another 550 men, Stanley assessed his fighting potential at 1,000 men, 100 of whom bore fire-arms. This minor army passed out of friendly Uganda into hostile Unyoro territory on January 2nd, 1876, and by January 11th was encamped on a plateau 1500 feet above Lake Edward.

January 12th, 1876:

Halt.

It was agreed with all hands concerned with our further progress, that this morning we were to descend from the plateau, on which we had camped, to the Lake shore and there construct a strong camp while Pocock and I put together the sections of the boat and make her fit for rough service on the Albert Nyanza [*L. Edward*] and the Wangwana fitted the canoe, which we had conveyed all the way from Uganda. At the end of 2 days I promised to have all things for departure. Meanwhile Sambuzi and I sent out some 500 men to select a feasible path or descent to the Lake shore from the plateau, as we heard that it was barely possible to convey the sections down after the ordinary method of the march as there was a precipice some 50 feet deep of most rugged rock. Late last night it was decided to halt one day more in our camp on the plateau while men went to search for a path by which the boat could be lowered down without damaging her, also to send out an expedition to seize upon all the canoes along the shore and after their seizure to decide upon a proper compensation to the owners for them. While these two expeditions numbering some 800 men altogether were gone upon their mission, a large force of natives were seen assembled to the east of the camp on the crest of a hill evidently reconnoitring. The great war drum was at once sounded, and the camps summoned to prepare for war. Sambuzi himself headed a large party and sallied out to meet them to see if their presence meant hostility, while I with 50 rifles took position on a hill to observe the field and to act as circumstances would demand.

As Sambuzi approached them, he was hailed and asked the cause of our invasion of their country. Sambuzi was instructed to inform them that we were friendly strangers come to see the Nyanza and that in 3 days we would depart, if permitted, as

109

peaceable as we had entered, but if obstructed in our work, or assaulted, we would defend ourselves as well as we could. "If you are friendly strangers," said they, "why do you come with guns and spears? Why have you not communicated with our King upon your object? No, no, you are liars, you are bad men. You Waganda have brought the White Man to eat the country" —that means to hold the country by force. To which Sambuzi replied: "Are we women that we should come with no arms to defend ourselves? If we are bad men, tell us what bad thing we have done. Have we captured your women and children or cattle? Have we burnt your houses? Have you seen any of us lift a spear against you? No. We are friends, and if you wait 3 days, you shall see for yourselves. We have not sent word to your King, because you all ran away [*at the first attempt to parley*], and if we had searched for you you would have said that we had come to war. We waited for you here, and now that you have come, go and carry our words to the King."

"No, we will not carry lies to the King, because he knows you are bad. The White Men of Kaniessa fight every day with Kabba Rega [*King of Unyoro*], and do you think that another white man coming behind his back comes in peace? We are not come to fight with you now, but tomorrow you will see us round you. It is true you have come, but tell us how you will get away from here. Can you fly in the air? If not, think of tomorrow and sleep on what we have told you."

After their departure Sambuzi called all his Chiefs and myself together to hold a Council, at which I was asked what I wished done. I told them that if they had forgotten the words of Mtesa, I had not, and that I wished for nothing more than what Mtesa had commanded them to do, *viz*, to proceed to the Lake shore and select a suitable place to build a camp, and then stop until I returned from my work on the Lake. They all at once returned a most determined answer that they would not, because they could not, because if they did they would all die and I should find on return nothing but the bones of the Waganda and the Wangwana who died fighting, because however strong their camp or stockade might be, they could not hold out a month against the three nations, the Wanyoro, Wanzimba and Wasagara. There was so much truth in this answer that though

110

I earnestly opposed their resolution for an hour it appealed to my commonsense and I therefore abandoned. Failing this, I proposed that we should do all in our power to get canoes, in which I could put the property of the Expedition, while the Wangwana could travel alongshore swiftly, loaded with their rifles only, while I could lead the canoes close ashore and follow them, and be at hand always to help them. This pleased Sambuzi, but just then the expeditions returned, and said that they had not been able to get one canoe as they had all been taken away to Kisera, an island in the middle of the Gulf. This project also failed, and was abandoned.

I next proposed that we should go down to the Lake, and proceed to build my boat and canoe, and promised that on the morning of the third day I would start on my journey and that they could depart for Uganda. This met with the approval of all, and all agreeing to start in the early morning for the Lake, the Council broke up. At 3 p.m., however, I noticed that the Waganda were tying and bundling up, and all preparing large stores of provisions of sweet potatoes and millet, as if they intended to take their departure in the night. My suspicions were strongly roused, and I instructed the more prudent of my people to proceed to question the Waganda in a careless manner as to what this preparation meant and it was soon discovered that they were going off as soon as the moon was up and leave the White man.

All my people discovered their project as soon as I did and they also caught the infection of departure and prepared to abscond in a body. Even the veterans of the Expedition, those who had accompanied me on my search after Livingstone and those who had accompanied that heroic traveller to his grave in Mullala were not proof against it. It was not abject cowardice which induced them to look blankly and despairingly on our position but the utter impossibility of seeing a way to extricate themselves from certain destruction. I called all these faithful men to my house and asked them to open their hearts to me, that I might give them my ideas. After a long hesitation, the gallant and ever faithful Kacheche spoke and said:

"Master, I don't know what my brothers here think of the pit in which I see we are fallen, but I would tell you truly what I think. I will do exactly what you say. Either live, or

111

die, all is one to me. If you say let us go on, I am ready; if you say return, I am with you; but I want you to tell me if we go on to the Lake, have we any chance at all to be able to start on our journey?

"Tomorrow there will be war, for Sambuzi and his Chiefs sent men out as soon as you left the Council, to spy out what the natives were doing. Half an hour ago the spies returned and said that young Rugi, the King of this country, is camped only 2 miles from us, between us and Uzimba Mountain over which the road leads from here to Uganda, and another force is south east of us, Wasagara shepherds, the spies say, because they have no other weapons than bows and arrows, and between us and the Lake, every village is full of people, and the hills all around are covered with men, and I have seen these myself as well as the Wangwana. Now, if the Waganda would but stop 2 days or even 1 day we could get off, I think, but if the Waganda will not stop, by remaining here alone to fight all these people is certain death. This is what is in my heart and I believe the cause of this panic among the Wangwana, but I am ready to do what you say. Only do tell us, do you see yourself any way to save the Expedition?"

Kacheche's words were, as I was told by the veterans, their opinion also.

"Well," said I, "there is no need of fear yet. Nobody is hurt, and there is no war. Let us all go to Sambuzi and we will know the truth of what you say."

We all went to Sambuzi whom we found with his chiefs in a state of great alarm.

As soon as I was seated, Sambuzi said: "Stamlee"—Kiganda construction for Stanley—"you are my friend, the King's friend, and the son of Uganda, and I want to do my duty towards you as well as I am able, but I must tell you the truth: we cannot do what you want us to do. We cannot wait here 2 days, nor 1 day. We shall fight tomorrow, that is certain, and if you think I speak from fear, you shall see me handle the spear. These people know me from past times and they know that my spear is heavy and sharp. We shall fight tomorrow as soon as the sun is well up, and we must cut our way through them to Uganda. We cannot fight and continue in our camp, for once the war is begun, it is war which will last as long as we stop

Camp at Mpwapwa—based on a drawing by the author.
Photograph: Richard Stauley

Mtesa's palace at Rubaga—from a drawing by the author.
Photograph: Richard Stanley

The Ripon Falls,
a sketch from the
author's notebook.
Richard Stanley

Mtesa I, the Kabaka
of Uganda, from
a photograph
by the author.
Richard Stanley

here until we are all dead, for these people take no slaves in war as the Waganda do. Then the only chance for life that we have is to pack up and have everything ready and fight our way through them. Now, what will you do? Will you stop here, or go with us and try another road? I must tell you if you do not know it yourself, that you will never put your boat in the Nyanza, if you stop here tomorrow. How can you get your boat down the cliffs while you are fighting and thousands pressing round you, and after you reach the water, how can you work on your boat 2 days while fighting? And what is the use of your boat in the water when your people are fighting their way on shore etc. etc."

Sambuzi was proceeding in this clever logical style setting forth numberless reasons for returning to Uganda, but none for remaining. Fear had so taken possession of their senses, that if I but hinted that there were as strong reasons for remaining as for returning, they were ready to get violently angry and regard me as an enemy. But I did venture on saying that if he remained 2 days, I would reward him even to the half of my property, to which he replied that he could not see the use of it when one was dead, even if I promised all. I, then, seeing that persuasion was useless with people overwhelmed with fear, said: "Do what you like then, we shall hear more of this again."

Early at dawn then we started, the natives stood on the hills watching, but not molesting us, and as we travelled over the summit of Mount Uzimba into the forest, they closed in on our rear keeping at a respectful distance soever, and so we trudged on to the camp on the Rusango River.

The trip to the Albert Nyanza [*L. Edward*] was not unsuccessful though the purpose of it was not effected. We reached the Lake, saw it, drank of its waters, and took an astronomical position of it 30° 37′ mins. E. Long. N. Lat. 27′. We had explored the land lying between the two Lakes, discovered the snow mountain of Gambaragara [*Mount Gordon-Bennett*] and the lofty mountains of Kabuga and Kibanga, traced the Katonga Lagoon to its utmost limits, and made the interesting discovery that a low hilly ridge about a mile and a half [*long*] forms the water-shed of rivers flowing into the Albert [*L. Edward*] and Victoria Nyanza, besides obtaining much interesting information of the countries bordering the route: Unyoro, Uzongora, Bwambu, Butwo and Ankori.

The Expedition then moved off again, its rearguard harried by the prudent but still hostile Wanyoro. On January 22nd Sambuzi and his forces left the Expedition for home, subtilising 180 pounds of Stanley's beads at their departure. Bull the bulldog died of fatigue and lack of meat. Despite messages from Mtesa inviting Stanley to return to court, Stanley decided, having experienced the Waganda enough, to pursue his journey and leave Uganda for ever, and marched resolutely south west in the general direction of Lake Tanganyika. On February 25th he reached the amenities of the Arab trading centre of Kafurro in the Kingdom of Karagwe, where he was comfortably housed within visiting distance of King Rumanika who was holding his court on the shores of a lake. The neighbouring Kingdom of Ruanda was an expanding power at the time.

February 27th:

Halt.
Paid a visit to King. Very well received. Fine old man about 55 or 60 years old. Clean shaved. Saw Ruanda handsome slender well-formed people.

February 28th:

Frank sent with boat to Lake to fix her up ready.

February 29th:

Halt.
Am sick from fever.

March 1st:

Arrive at Nyanza, or Lake of Rumanika [*named Lake Windermere by Speke*]. Give revolver and ammunition, 30 cloths and 1 cap to King. King sends a guide to show me the various points on Lake. [*These included the mouth of the Kagera River.*]

March 8th:

Slept last night in the Kagera, drawing the boat among the papyri. The boats were left on floating masses of these reeds, fuel was supplied by dried papyri, stones for the cooking pots had substitutes in long papyrus stalks driven like piles into the raft. Beds were made of the broom-like tops. Were it not for the hordes of voracious mosquitoes, we might have passed the night very well. Arrived at 9 a.m. this day at Kazinga, a point of land extending about a mile from the base of the mountain on the Karagwe side into the Kagera valley. The Kagera with its swampy marges is about 5 or 6 miles wide. From the Cape we see that the Kagera extends from mountain to mountain 6 miles apart and maintains the same breadth from Kishakka to Ishango. Food was reluctantly supplied gratis by a poor population.

March 9th:

Soon after leaving Kazinga, we left river and by a branch entered into an open river-like water. Arrive at Unyamubi. Kishakka, Uvari and Ishango, Ruanda has taken now, so that all are included under the title of Ruanda. South of Ruanda is Urundi. Kagera runs between Urundi and Ruanda.

Returning to Kafurro, Stanley next marched 35 miles north-wards to observe a local curiosity, the hot springs of Mtagata.

March 15th:

Mtagata hot springs. Tested the hot water. Springs 6 in number. At the extreme source $129\frac{1}{2}$°F. Where people bathe 110°F. People from Ngoi, Iwanda, Mpororo, Kiziwa come here to bathe. People sick from ulcerous sores, itch, bathing here. On extreme left 107°F. springs bubble up, others issue out in streams. If the place were cleaned and the springs united in one large bathing pond it would be better.

Stanley bottled some of the water, conveyed it safely across Africa, round the Cape and eventually to London where he submitted it to Messrs. Savory and Moore, 143 Bond Street, for chemical and micro-chemical analysis. The water proved to be faintly alkaline in property.

On March 19th Stanley arrived back in Kafurro; he visited King Rumanika's treasure house, made an inventory of his own provisions and set out again on March 25th with 3 of Rumanika's men to guide him to the land of the King's sons 68 miles towards the south west.

March 30th:

. . . Arrived at Uhimba.

Uhimba is governed by three sons of Rumanika, Kakoka, Kananga and Ruhinda and in all my experience in Africa I met with none to equal these for begging: tins and iron boxes, guns, powder, pepper, English cloth, blankets etc. until I could do no more but simply smile in a blank manner at their pertinacity and my own inability to satisfy these young sharks.

Leaving these blades so unlike their saintly, generous father, Stanley, though feverish, marched another 57 miles.

April 10th:

On this day we have crossed the last of these stupendous ridges between which nature has furrowed or scooped out deep valleys to conceive the lusty roaring streams that run north-east and south-west, to the Nile and the Congo.

The water shed at which the Nile and the Congo are born is hardly 2 miles wide from base to base. On the north-west side near Kafurro, one of the effluents of the Victoria, the Lohugati is born; on the south eastern side whence spreads the valley of Uyagoma, a small stream oozes slowly among reeds and rushes—it is one of the sources of the Malagarazi, the principal effluent of the Tanganyika.

The rocks of these ridges are all of the primitive kind, but of no particular character. Iron taints the clays, as well as the rocks. In the latter it is seen as solid lumps, large masses, *scoriae*, or winds in irregular lines among the strata. At the head waters of the Meruzi in north-east Uhha, I saw some large masses of fine white quartz at Uhimba. I saw several small hills of red and white veined steatite. Porphyry is abundant and some sandstone, granite, and gneiss were about; strata perpendicular and generally following the ridges in their course north east and south west.

Another 53 miles saw the Expedition at the capital of the youthful King of Urangwa.

April 18*th & * 19*th:*

Halt.
Paid 6 *doti* to King and received a bullock. We have halted here because we have heard that Mirambo is advancing upon Serombo. The appearance of such a notorious robber naturally creates excitement throughout the country. He, however, declares he has come on peaceful business, but prudence compelled us to wait a little before proceeding further.

Hamed Ibrahim, my friend at Kafurro, has in store here about 900 *fraslah* of ivory—over 14 tons—over $90,000 in value at Zanzibar. Rather an imprudence for a man to risk his all in the keeping of the King of Urangwa.

April 20*th:*

Marched to Serombo. South-east by East 10 miles.
. . . Tonight we hear Brown Besses, or as they are called here the "Gumeh Gumeh", roar to announce the dread Mirambo's approach. It is said he comes tomorrow. The crier of the King has gone about crying: "Tomorrow dig potatoes, dig potatoes tomorrow, Mirambo comes, therefore dig potatoes, potatoes, dig potatoes" [*to feast and appease his troops*].

April 21*st:*

Halt.
Mirambo entered Serombo today with the state that ought to belong to such a notorious Chief in Central Africa. The Brown Besses and Tower Muskets charged with about $\frac{1}{2}$ [*pound*] of powder roared like cannon and were fired at regular intervals during the entire advance and entry into Serombo. About 20 drums also beat a welcome and the Wanyamwezi women, previously schooled, set up a shrill and prolonged lululuing.

Later in the day he sent to beg a gun or pistol from me and prohibited my departure tomorrow until we had made friends.

Old Hickory's saying that he preferred boys to men for war was repeated today by one of Mirambo's Chiefs, who stated that it was Mirambo's saying: "We never take middle aged men or old men to our wars, always youths not yet troubled with wives or children. They have keener eyes and lither limbs for advance or retreat, and it takes but little to give them lion-hearts. In all our wars with the Arabs, they were youths who gave me victory. Fifteen of our boys died at one spot for the sake of one piece of red cloth. No, no. Give me youths for the forest but men for the *boma* or the fenced village."

April 22nd:

Halt.

This day will be memorable for the visit of the famous Mirambo to me accompanied by his Chiefs. He was so different from all I ever conceived of such a redoubtable chieftain and a bandit of such terrible reputation. A man 5 feet 11 inches in height, about 35 years old, well-made but with not an ounce of superfluous flesh about him; handsome, regular featured, mild, soft spoken, with what you would call a meek demeanour, generous, open-handed with nothing of the small cent ideas of narrow mean-minded men. Indeed I did not let myself readily believe that this could possibly be the ferocious Chief of the terrible Ruga-Ruga. I could not believe it until all the Arabs testified to it, for I had expected to see something of the Mtesa type—a man whose exterior would proclaim the man's life and rank—but this unpresuming quiet-eyed man of inoffensive meek exterior, whose language was so mild without a single gesture, indicated nothing of the Napoleonic genius which he has for 5 years displayed in the heart of Africa to the injury of Arabs and commerce and the nearly trebling the price of ivory. Nothing, I said, but I will except the eyes, which were composed and a steady calm gaze. And unlike all other Africans I have met, they met your own and steadily and calmly confronted them. Thus I had seen Mirambo.

At night I was sent for to his tent, a bell tent 20 feet high and 25 feet in diameter, where we made brotherhood by an incision in each other's right leg above the knee until a couple of drops of blood were drawn; which interchanged and rubbed with butter, the Miryamwezi repeated a solemn curse on me if I proved faithless to the friendship: "May the lion devour you, the serpent poison you, bitterness be your food, your friends desert you, your gun wound yourself, and everything bad worry you until death."

My chief Captain pronounced a like curse on Mirambo. My new brother then gave 15 cloths as presents to my Chiefs, trebling my present to his people and to him.

Sayid bin Mohammed, a short quick loud-spoken young Arab, gave a bar of soap and a bag of pepper and saffron to me. I must try to remember him for his generous offers and assistance to a stranger.

April 23rd:

Mirambo at [*my*] departure accompanied me outside the gate and gave me 5 men to ensure my passing through the country without extortion . . .

Advancing 78 *miles through territory infested by rapacious chieftains, freebooters, and bandits of the wandering Watuta, Stanley heard tell of a French trader in the area and also received on May 2nd a present at long range of 4 bullocks and two milch-cows with calves, promised by his new friend and patron the super-brigand Mirambo at their leave-taking ten days earlier.*

May 3rd:

Halt [*at Ubagwe*].
Made a present to Mirambo of one pistol and 100 cartridges. Sent a note to the French trader at Urambo [*Mirambo's capital*] requesting some castor oil, some Epsom salts, bicarbonate of soda and a little sugar.

The Expedition marched 48 *miles.*

May 9th:

Crossed an inundated plain 1 mile wide. Robert came back with answer from M. Broyon, Swiss trader at Urambo. Brought 2 bars of Castile soap, one bottle castor oil and some *Figaros* of November and December, 1875. Sent a letter back to him with a sketch map of Victoria Nyanza and best ivory countries.

Such was the prestige of Mirambo and his Ruga-Ruga brigands that the local "big heads" with a taste for robbery with violence all claimed to be Ruga-Ruga whether they were or not. Stanley encountered a group of these toughs 63 *miles further on his way.*

May 17th:

Halt [*at Zogi*].

. . . [*So-called*] Ruga-Ruga in abundance, such smoking of *Banghi* such wild screaming and stormy sneezing never was heard, varied as they were with the everlasting day and night enduring monotone of the native guitar and hiccupy snorting vocal music.

Leaving these hemp-addicted Teddie-boys without reluctance, the Expedition marched another 105 miles and sighted the waters of Lake Tanganyika at noon on May 27th. At 3 p.m. Stanley was standing on the town square of Ujiji where he had so momentously encountered David Livingstone in November, 1871.

May 27th:

Arrived for the second time at Bunder Ujiji, but neither white man nor letters from Europe greet me this time. Muini Kheri, Mohammed bin Gharib are still here. Mohammed bin Sali is dead. Nothing is changed much except the everchanging mud *tembes*; the hills are everlasting, the Liuche continues its course, the Lake expands with the same beauty. The opposite mountains still look blue-black as ever, the surf still beats noisily as ever, the sun shines as bright, the sky is blue, but from the fact that the imposing central figure of the human group drawn together to meet me in Ujiji in 1871 is absent, Ujiji in spite of the beauty of its Lake and the greenness of its palms, seems strangely forlorn and uninteresting.

May 28th:

Halt at Kewele, Bunder Ujiji. Visits and congratulations.

May 29th:

Halt.

I have observed that the Lake is several feet higher than it was in November 1871. It is from the fact of the rains being very great this year. It is at least 250 yards inshore now to what it was then.

I received a large mass of bitumen from Muini Kheri. It is said to come from Ubari. Natives say it comes from above precipitated by lightning. Great quantities are sometimes found floating on the Lake. It is called by the Arabs *lalum* or pitch.

From May 28th to June 5th, the Explorer halted at Ujiji and devoted his notebook to the recording of temperatures, boiling points, latitudes, longitudes, altitudes and other scientific and mathematical observations. After two days ill in bed, Stanley began his circumnavigation of Lake Tanganyika on June 11th, sailing south along the eastern coast. Apart from general exploration, he was anxious to discover if any river flowed out of the Lake.

June 17th:

Voyage continues.

Camping at Bongo Island we were visited in the night by the robbers of Ndereh, who were drawn here by a lying report from the timid natives that we had attacked the village (Island) and bound the women captives. Though they found the report to be a mere fabrication, they took the opportunity to mulct us of 2 cloths. We paid it, and taking advantage of a quarrel amongst themselves shoved-off and avoided further mischief.

Three days later Stanley saw further evidence of the depredations of the Ndereh robbers at the recently sacked village of Kiwesa.

June 19th:

Voyage continues from Ulambula Cape to Kabogo Island.

Kabogo Island, a low island length of [*form?*] following the bends of the mainland at a distance of from 300 to 500 yards. On both shores flourish the borassus palm. At a distance of two or three miles the background is formed by a lofty mountainous ridge about 2,000 feet high. The robbers of Ndereh have caused Ponda or Kiata to move his village 3 days further south, so that the Point is now unoccupied. About this region wild game is abundant, elephant, buffalo, waterbuck and eland with zebra. They graze boldly along the water edge and up to this day I have succeeded in bagging 3 zebra and 1 antelope.

June 20th:

Paid a visit to Ponda's village, having to pass through it to get to leeward of some waterbuck which I intended to shoot. Found the fences all burnt. About 50 huts still standing unharmed by fire, traces of a recent conflict and hasty flight were abundant, dead men speared, stools, mats, drinking gourds, cooking vessels, *pombé* [*beer*] pots, walking sticks and clubs strew the ground. The Sultan's quarters were untouched. Twenty-five skulls grinned horribly before the door, 5 more were laid in a row a few paces in front of it on the ground. A portion of the town was still in perfect order. Reed fences surrounding some great man's hut and houses, doors of houses closed as if their owners had just left them for a visit to their neighbours. We were almost tempted to believe that the abandonment was but a ruse to trap unwary visitors, but blood, dried and black, proved that the abandonment was compulsory. The only living inhabitant that we saw was an immense black cat, so fat that she could scarcely run. The boatmen made very free with the loot and carried off about 50 sleeping mats, a score or so of good cooking pots, stools and cooking vessels and gourds. Ditch round it in some parts 10 feet deep and the excavated material thrown [*up*] in the most defensible village yet seen.

On subsequent days the voyage continued round the Lake, the Explorer calculating latitude and longitude, mean temperature, distances between points, taking soundings and appreciating the natural beauty of the scene. On June 26th one of his men had the misfortune to wound himself with his own Snyder and on the same day they crossed Livingstone's route at Bisa on his last journey and Stanley was shown the place where Livingstone had camped. On June 29th their boats floated over a submerged village. The water was 3 feet deep over the former fence or boma and the place was called Wanpembe . . . Submerged islands and so forth, bore witness to the surprising rise in the waters of the Lake, and suggested that there was no effluent from the Lake, which indeed proved to be the case.

On July 7th the Expedition experienced a tremendous gale but the voyage continued peacefully enough with chartings and calculations of the coast.

July 10th:

Voyage continues from camp 2 miles south of Lunangwa to Mamwende.

Last night see fire at the base of a lofty mountain. Soon the fire had surrounded the foot and creeping with speed [*up*] the steep face of the mountain within an hour was seen triumphant on the summit like a magnificent crown.

Close observation of this fire has taught me that the several plains broad and narrow along route from Coast devoid of trees and shrubs, save only a few ugly stalks of vegetable life, are caused by these fires. Wherever ground retains sufficient moisture, it produces accordingly a growth of grass more or less dense. In Africa this grass, in some places well nourished by depth of soil and moisture, attains the height and thickness of cane. Two months after the rains, this grass becomes dry as tinder; the smallest spark set to it, and the noise of battle between two Army Corps would not exceed the terrible racking, crackling, bursting noise made by the onrush of this windswept element. While it devours everything that stood before it, it has also roasted to a certain depth the earth which nourished the grass. The effects of the fire are burning stumps, blackened plain and a gaping fissured earth.

The record continues with sketch maps and calculations of the coasts of the Lake until on July 15th Stanley's party camped at the mouth of the Lukuga River:

While the sight is before me, I will endeavour to catch the spirit of the scene to convey to others somewhat of the impression it has made upon me. On our arrival here last night we found a slave caravan just arrived from Marungu about eleven or twelve hundred slaves owned by Salim bin Sayf, Habaje, Chief of Kewele and other Ujiji chiefs. Though the distance they had traversed was about 10 days' journey, it had made fearful havoc in their numbers and condition, from the fact that little or no food could be purchased for so many souls; for with the usual improvidence attending the buyer—Arab or native— when he finds a good thing, he will buy it to the fullest extent of his means, little thinking of the means left to carry his wares to Ujiji sound and safe. The consequence was in this case that numbers had died, especially children, from insufficient nourishment. The surviving children were in a condition ill-resembling humanity. The chests jutted out with the protuberence of a skeleton frame, while the poor bellies were in such a fearfully attenuated state like an empty bladder; ribs and bones glared out; legs were mere sticks of bone, trembling weak supports to the large head and large chest. As they were embarked, each slave gang, chained, pushed on in the rear by those still behind, fearful of their impatient masters, uttered their prayers and remonstrances to those ahead in the most piteously querulous tones, common to querulous sick people.

The elders were in chains, but the number was so great that heavy bark cords had been made to which the slaves were strung by the neck a few foot apart. Even children few years old were subjected to the same treatment, probably because it was easier to count the list by gangs than one by one.

Many of the older males were quite new to this servile treatment, as was evinced by downcast heads and abashed faces when strangers looked at them.

July 22nd:

. . . The guns sold to the Wanyamwezi by the Arabs for slaves and ivory have transformed them into many detachments of banditti. Stern depopulation goes forward.

Fired by avarice and blood, whole hosts of masked, armed Wanyamwezi ravage and depopulate extensive lands, and drive despairing files of slaves to the Arab markets. Ivory is precious and scarce, but slaves are plentiful, women are prolific and swarm in the interior, and there are broad lands where people are disunited, have many chiefs, and consequently are weak, and fall easy prey before crackling fusillades of musketry which awake in midnight hours from slumber. As far as Kataka, they carry their blood-red banners after the Arab style, massacring the old, enslaving the young. They meet checks sometimes, but these but drive them to other corners, and it was by one of these checks they were driven to Marungu where they have reaped and are still reaping an unexampled forest.

The voyage continued uneventfully.

July 27th:

Waganga Ubwari.

Yesterday after exploring to the end of Burton Bay, we coasted along the Masansi shore, and at each large village lowered sail and made enquiries about rivers etc, according to custom. On coming near a village on the west bank of the Kasansagara River, we were forewarned by the female natives flying wildly away loaded with articles, of a rude reception. But approaching nearer we were told by the Wabembe cannibals not to advance unless we desired war. Wishing to test how far they would venture without sufficient provocation, I motioned the boats to advance. From wild gestures, striking spears on the ground, beating the water, and hopping up and down, they turned to stones of such large size as might well be termed dangerous missiles. Motioning a halt, we quietly surveyed the natives, watched the rocks flying into the air making deep pits in the water as they fell, like at an entertainment specially got up for our amusement. Not a word, a sign or a movement on our part indicated either wrath or pleasure, until the natives, as if tired, made a pause and regarded each other with encouragement. For my part I remembered the gentle-souled Livingstone and told them, if they were not such fools, I could feel hearty anger, but we had nothing to say to people who treated strangers so rudely without cause.

We tried to make a camp at Kiunyu, Chief Mahonga's land. As we spoke they mocked us. When we asked them if they would sell some grain, they asked us if they were our slaves that they should till their land and sow grain for us. Meanwhile, canoes were launched and criers sent ahead to proclaim that we were coming. The beach was crowded with infuriates and mockers. Perceiving that a camp was hopeless in this vicinity, we pulled off, but having gone about half a mile, we perceived we were followed by several canoes in some of which we saw spears shaken at us. We halted and made ready, and as they approached still in this hostile fashion, I opened on them with the Winchester Repeating Rifle. Six shots and four deaths were sufficient to quiet the mocking etc. etc. etc. and to establish a different character for ourselves—somewhat more respectable, if not more desirable. We captured three canoes, some fish and nets etc. as spoil. I had an opportunity also to prove that although able to resent affronts and meet hostility we were not inhuman nor revengeful, for a wounded man struggling to escape from dread decapitation—the common fate of the wounded in battle—cried out for mercy and the rifle was lowered and he was permitted to go. We then proceeded on our way . . .

On July 29th they sailed round once more into the territory of Ujiji which they reached at 6 a.m. after a night voyage of 12 hours rowing, and continued by stages until they reached Ujiji itself on July 31st, thus completing an 810 mile circuit of the Lake in 51 days.

The record then falls silent until August 21st, 1876, by which time preparations for the last and most daring phase of the Anglo-American Expedition were well in hand.

PART IV

LAKE TANGANYIKA—THE ATLANTIC OCEAN

August 1876—August 1877

LAKE TANGANYIKA—THE ATLANTIC OCEAN

Until Stanley set out from Ujiji on August 25th, 1876, he had not been travelling in totally unexplored lands, but henceforth, once he left the trails of Livingstone (1866–73) and Cameron (1873–75) at Nyangwe, 87 miles west of Lake Tanganyika, his explorations of the headwaters of the River Congo and its course to the Atlantic were uniquely his own. His two problems were first to identify this great river in its infancy among the multitudinous streams of Terra Incognita, and then, having established its identity, to follow it through appalling hazards to the mouth of its vast estuary.

The day before his departure he made an inventory of his remaining possessions:

Shells and beads	—	29	loads
Cloth	—	8	loads
Salt	—	1	load
Medicine	—	1½	loads
Fat	—	2	loads
Rice and Flour	—	2	loads
Tea	—	1	load
Books	—	1	load
Bed	—	1	load
Powder boxes	—	11	loads
etc. etc.			

95 loads in all.

As Ujiji lay on the eastern shore of Lake Tanganyika, Stanley's first task was to ferry the Expedition across to the western shore. This he organised in two parts, the advance party leaving on August 30th, Stanley and the rear echelon coming up with them on September 4th and the united forces halting at Mtowa, the Arab crossing place in the district of Uguhha, to re-organise.

September 5th:

Sick in bed of remittent fever. Frank in the evening sent back to Ujiji to recover if possible some runaways.

September 6th:

Sick in bed—fever.

September 7th:

Fever broke off at midnight. Recover but terribly weak.

September 8th:

Halt at Arab Crossing or Mtowa.
Am nearly well, thank God. Have begun to unscrew the boat.

September 9th:

Halt at Arab crossing.
Distributed loads. Heat this month terrible—138°F. in the sun.

September 12th:

Halt.
The White man in the opinion of the Waguhha:
"How can he be a good man who comes for no trade, whose feet you never see, who always goes covered with clothes, unlike all other people? No, there is something very mysterious about him, perhaps wicked, perhaps he is a magician, at any rate it is better to leave him alone and not disturb him."

September 13th:

Halt.
Frank returns from Ujiji (8 days) bringing with him 4 deserters.

September 14th:

Marched to Ruanda 6½ miles.
Kalulu deserted for no known reason . . .

September 15th:

Halt.
Kalulu was arrested today by the detective Kacheche and aides, who had fled to Kasenge Island where he was found

negotiating for a passage to Ujiji. Paid 5 *doti* for his apprehension . . .

The Expedition continued uneventfully and Stanley noted that the journey had lasted from September 16th until October 6th, 21 days, 200½ miles at 9½ miles day. *The march continued.*

On October 15th he reached Mtuyu, 55 miles further, and noted:

From Kabungwe to Mtuyu country very populous, enough villages if peopled with brave men to have made a brigade to proceed with caution. The people, however, did not attempt to molest us, though an enormous number followed us, led by curiosity to see our asses, and to know whether they were to regard us as friends or foes.

In some places in Manyema we were called sons of cows. In others Wasambye. By the latter name is meant the Arabs and slaves and all people wearing cloth [*cotton*]—it is full of terror to a great many tribes. In other places we were called Nivema or Whites.

October 16th:

Marched to Mpungu 15 miles West.

We skirt the range of hills which bound the broad Luama Valley on the north. People excessively timid. We have seen no women since we crossed the Luama. Those of Kabungwe when questioned as to whither all the women had gone exclaimed pathetically with an action expressive of distress and grief: "Our women are all dead, all cut off, every one. It was the smallpox! Only men are left now in Kabungwe!" Some of our enterprising people roving and foraging about discovered several in a wooded gully.

Kitete, Chief of Mpungu, has a beard which he twists 18 inches long. Six or 7 blue glass beads ended the lengthy beard. His brother has one 6 inches long. There were others of unusual length 3 or 4 inches. He bore as his insignia of office a huge Hercules club, blackened with fire. He presented me with a goat and I gave him 40 shells—Cowries.

There was a wood at Kabungwe which was very offensive. The odour made the village almost unbearable. On being used for fuel, it emitted a smell putrid and foul, and a good deal of oily matter.

October 17th:

Marched to Mkwanga, Uzura West-north-west 12 miles.

After 4 miles march we came to where the Luama conflowed with the mighty river Lualawa, Lualaba or Ugarowa. Islands were seen in it. Across river was a low valley, open country unmarked with any peculiar eminence or elevation except Kijima 2000 feet above the valley. After reaching the end of the range which bounded the Luama Valley on the north, we turned north westerly and entered Uzura. Whence we followed the course of the Lualaba as far as Lulindi River. At Mkwanga we met two Wangwana from Kasonga who gave us news of the late massacre of an entire [*Arab*] caravan on the road to Kasesa by Manyema treachery, and of the departure of Tippu-Tib—Hamed Hamudi—to avenge the massacre.

October 18th:

Marched 18 miles North by West.

By spurring our men we made a brilliant march and crossed the broad and uninhabited plain which separates Uzura from Tubanda district. Heartily welcomed by Arabs and natives. Saw the redoubted Hamed bin Mohammed *alias* Tippu-Tib, a fine handsome dark man of Arab extraction in the prime of life, who next to Sayid bin Habib is the first of Arab explorers. To him Cameron is indebted for many courtesies, he accompanied him with over 200 muskets as far as Utotera South Lat 5° Long. 25°54′, then to Jumah Merikani in Rua he sent 2 guides.

Jumah Merikani was one more of a number of prominent Arabs to have penetrated and settled in Central Africa in the course of the previous thirty years.

Between October 19th and October 22nd the Explorer worked out an agreement with Tippu-Tib that the latter should escort the Expedition through the Rain Forest. The substance of what was agreed on October 22nd falls under six headings, as follows:

1. Sixty camps to commence from opposite Nyangwe in any direction I choose.

2. To be permitted if I decide in striking to the West Coast with a caravan to take as many men and guns as necessary for my defence.

3. That $5,000 and food for 140 men shall cover all expenses except such rewards as I choose to make voluntarily.

4. Sixty camps not to exceed 3 months, the rate of march to be 2 marches and 1 halt.

5. The 60 camps to be in a westerly direction—exclusive of return.

6. Each march to be 4 hours in length, provisions to be begun distributing on crossing the Lualaba, and ended at Nyangwe [*on completion 3 months later*].

October 23rd:

Marched to Marimbu North-west 11 miles.

October 24th:

Marched North-west-north 13 miles Benangongo.

A fine rolling pastoral country but depopulated and sadly marked by many a ruined village—the mutual work of treachery and cowardice opposed by revengeful cruelty, spurred on by avarice.

The Expedition reached Nyangwe on October 26th.

October 28th:

Halt.

A terrible sandstorm blew from south south-east this afternoon.

Kalulu was shot by accident with Mabruki Manyapara's gun at Kankumba [*on October 25th*]. Bullet passed through inner right thigh, passed through fleshy part of left side glancing a rib. Kalulu was then lying down.

During the halt the Explorer had time to note that the wealthy Arab called Abed bin Salim was the possessor of two large English hens with fine broods of young ones. Also, that the soil of Nyangwe was fatal to onions because of worms which destroy them.

November 5th:

Start from Nyangwe North-north-east to Nakasimbi, district of Nyangwe. Marched 9½ miles for 3½ hours.

Hamed bin Mohammed *alias* Mtibula, or Tippu-Tib, accompanied by nearly 500 souls and over 200 fighting men which, added to our party, make a list of about 700 souls. Muini Kibwana and several young Arabs accompany him. Tippu-Tib is the most dashing and adventurous Arab that has ever entered Africa and to ensure success in this exploration I could not have done better than to have secured his aid in exploring a dangerous country. Few tribes will care to dispute our passage now. I look forward in strong hopes to do valuable explorations. From Nyangwe here travelled over a fine rolling plain-like country, crossed one stream going east.

November 6th:

Mpotira. Nyangwe district North ½ East 12 miles.
We had our first experience of the woods, damp and rotting trees and bushes, though there had been no rain.

November 7th:

Halt at Mpotira, to allow a winding caravan under our escort to come up with hundreds of sheep and goats which they are taking to Tata for trade. A sheep is said to purchase one ivory, 12 slaves purchase an ivory. In Ujiji 6 slaves purchase an ivory.
"Slaves cost nothing," said Hamed bin Mohammed, "they only require to be gathered." And that is the work of Muini Dugumbi and Mtagamoyo [*Tippu-Tib's freebooting companions*].
These half-castes of Nyangwe have no cloth or beads or wares of merchandise. They obtain their ivory by robbing. It is the story of sea pirates and buccaneers over again, of Captain Black the Buccaneer. They attack the simple peoples of Nyangwe right and left, 12 or 15 slaves then caught are sold for 35 pounds of ivory. Muini Dugumbi has one hundred to one hundred and twenty women. Mtagamoyo has 60 . . .

November 8th:

North ½ West 9 miles to district of Karindi, Uregga.
We had a fearful time of it today in the woods—such crawling, scrambling, tearing through the damp cool jungles, with such height and depth of woods. Once we got a sidelong view

from the limited crown of a hill over the wild woods around us which swept in irregular waves towards the Lualaba and of green grass plains on the other side of the Lualaba. It was a wild and weird scene. It was so dark sometimes that I could not see easily the words I wrote in my field book.

November 9th:

North ½ West 10½ miles to Kiussi.

Another difficult day's work in the forest and jungle. Our caravan is no longer the tight compact force which was my pride, but utterly disorganised; each one scrambling to the best of his ability through the woods. The boat bearers were utterly wearied out. It may be said we cut our way through. The vanguard armed with axes and bill-hooks performed hard work, but to make a road like the pioneers of a governmental army would require many days, as prostrate giants with a mountain of branches and twigs would have to be cut through. To save time we were obliged to cut roads winding round these vast obstructions.

The question which agitates my mind is: whether it would be best to follow the Lualaba to the sea; or follow the Lualaba north until it turns west, and then strike for Munza's thus joining Livingstone's and Schweinfurth's discoveries.

If I struck for the sea, a terrible puzzle presents itself. What shall I do with my people? They would be unable to return overland to Zanzibar, and *The Herald* and *Telegraph* would never undertake to incur the expense of sending the party by sea round the Cape. And the glory of crossing Africa would be small for a second party immediately after Cameron's.

On the other hand, by going to Munza's I resolve the problem of the Lualaba, I round the sources of the Nile, and it is better for the interests of my employers; I could discharge my men at Gondoroko and they could return in safety to Zanzibar via Uganda.

However, I leave these questions to be decided definitely until some 30 camps ahead, when I must resolve what I mean to do. I must also have an eye for my supplies for they are diminishing rapidly.

The squall heralding rain raises a noise above our heads like that of storm waves driven against rocks.

This was particularly disheartening country for the porters carrying the dismantled boat and over the next 14 miles they lagged behind alarmingly.

November 12th:

Halt.

It has been decided to abandon the right bank of the Lualaba, there is no food sufficient for our force to be found in the jungles and the jungle forest is too dense to make way. However, for 18 camps ahead I have obtained a pretty correct knowledge. We shall follow the Lualaba on the left bank. Boat came today, people utterly fagged out and disheartened.

November 13th:

Wenekamankua North $\frac{1}{4}$ West 4 miles.
Still woods, woods, woods.

November 14th:

Marched to Wane-Mbeza, Uregga. 8 miles still through the forest North-west.

Uregga it seems runs like a broad belt from north-north-east to south-south-west. Its people know nothing beyond three camps on either side. Many of them have not even seen the Lualaba River, though they are but 30 miles off. The most incurious people ever met. They have been imprisoned for generations in their woods, and the difficulty of making way through these forests which surround them is the sole cause why they know nought of the world outside or the world outside knows aught of them. It appears to be synonymous with the Forest Country.

Woods and deep ravines with an outlook towards the north and north-east of a world of hills and ranges of the most portentous and forbidding kind. To add to our toilsome situation, Hamed bin Mohammed, labouring uneasily under his contract, first found fault with the length of the marches, and then wished to bind me down with a promise that at the end of 60 camps I should give him one half of my force to enable him to return to Nyangwe, whether I saw means or not of being able to proceed towards the confluence of the Lualaba and the Coango.

As this was sheer nonsense to reduce my force in the middle of the wilderness, without the slightest prospect of overcoming the difficulty of proceeding to fulfil my mission, the proposal was not entertained but I endeavoured to keep him within the terms of the agreement. This he refused to do, because after escorting me so far he would be afraid to return alone with only his own people. The natives—he said—would suspect he had fought in some country and they would, roused by cupidity or blood-thirstiness, set on us with the cry "Let's finish them!". No, he could not think of it. "Give me," said he, "30 or 35 guns and men at the end of the 60 camps and I will go with you that distance."

While I wished him to proceed according to the contract, on the promise that should I meet with a Portuguese caravan, I should give him 30 or 35 guns and men, while I should proceed with 15 or 20 men on my way; or if at the end of the 60 camps, provided such distance approached anywhere near the confluence of the two rivers Coango and Lualaba, if he would wait, I would leave half my goods in his possession and with my force I would push on rapidly to where the two rivers flowed and contented with the work done would return with him to Nyangwe, and thence to Zanzibar. No, the Arab, whose mind was bent on breaking the agreement or making money, refused to listen. He seemed bent on making the marches as short as possible by delays and needless waits on the road, so that the 60 marches would not indeed amount to more than 30 ordinary marches.

The River Coango (Kuango) is a large tributary of the R. Congo, though at that time Stanley had no exact idea where it was.

November 16th:

Halt.
Hamed bin Mohammed alias Tippu-Tib has broken the contract and has suggested a new one, which as I cannot better myself I must accept, namely: he agrees to escort me to Kima-Kima on the Rumami River.

November 17th:

Marched 11 miles North-west Kampunzu.

Still woods—most frightful work. We have left Uregga, and entered Uvinza or Uzimba, who wear caps of monkey skin, heavy red copper rings round ankles. Weapons: a short bladed spear, a knife and small bows which shoot poisoned arrows: bows are not more than about a foot in length, for they are only to wound at short distance. The slightest wound occasions death if blood drawn, powerful poison. A variety of trees and shrubs, perfectly wonderful. The cotton woods serve for boards to make doors. They carve long benches, low stools. Red woods also abundant and a tough black wood resembling ebony forms the favourite spear staff. Village of Kampunzu is about 500 yards long, one street 30 feet wide forms the village, clay walls. Waregga use wattled walls.

Blood brotherhood is a sure sign of peace. This was made between Frank Pocock and the Chief, and interchanged presents.

Women of Uregga and Uzimba are naked. Men wear a loin clout of bark cloth or grass cloth. The bark cloth tree is almost a sure indication of the duration of each settlement. In Uganda, where peace is ensured by force and numbers, they grow to a great size hundreds of years old. But in all these sections I have failed to see trees more than 30 or 40 years old.

November 19th:

March 5 miles West to Lualaba River East Long. 26° 12' S. Lat. 3° 35'.

Arrived at river—which is divided into two broad streams 60 yards wide by a series of small wooded islands—we began to screw up the boat and make arrangements for crossing. We endeavoured, before they were aware we had a boat, to bargain for canoes, but such obtuse-headed fellows jeered us, requested us to give them a heap of shells a cubit high, which would have been about 140 pounds. We proceeded quietly with our work and suddenly launched the boat amid shouts, and manning her with 25 rifles appeared behind the islands in front of the Wagenya settlements and proceeding close to the bank commanded them to appear at camp before sunset to make friends, or we should make war on them. By 5 p.m. we had crossed 150 men into the island in front from the eastern bank. This fact, it seems, acted on the natives with greater force for they at once appeared with canoes to assist the crossing. Had we not had the boat we should have had to wait a month.

At Kampunzu's we saw what appeared to us each street or village lined with human skulls. One had 26, another 10, another 13, which made us first imagine Kampunzu as a terrible fighter, but we were told that they were Sokos' or gorillas' skulls singularly resembling humanity—4½ feet high, the size of a lad of 14 or thereabouts, hair black brown and long. I offered Kampunzu a high price if he would show me one dead or alive, but though he beat the drum and started scores off to hunt, he was unsuccessful.

November 20th:

Crossed Lualaba at Rukonbeh's, 458 souls, 4 asses and about 150 loads of beads and cloth etc. etc. The natives could not be induced to assist, and we had to take canoes by force. No violence was however used. Notwithstanding we offered high prices for food, natives ran away abandoning everything.

November 21st:

Halt.

We have used all the diplomacy in our power to induce the natives to be friends, but it has been of no use. Two of my people went to purchase food. The natives sold food but in the meantime surrounded them and one of them threw a spear at Kacheche, who shot him dead. There is not a native within 10 miles of us.

Stanley and the more intrepid boarded the boats while the remainder of the Expedition followed down-river on land with Tippu-Tib.

November 22nd:

Floated down Lualaba as far as confluence of Ruiki with Lualaba about 1½ knots from 7 a.m. to 12. From 1.30–4.30 p.m. the natives spread the alarm as soon as we came in sight. At Makula's, however, they were holding a market and no-one noticed our approach until we were within two hundred yards. Then a little child ran up the river bank and seemed to ask his mother: "What strangers we were"; which she no sooner saw than she screamed: "The Wasambye, the Wasambye" in an agony of alarm. At the dread name the market dissolved. We heard rushes through the bush by panicky women and children, as if a herd of buffaloes were distractedly driven by a fly pest. The drum which we had heard five hours upstream was silenced. The goats which were quietly browsing near, at once appeared to feel the alarm and bounced off after their frightened owners. Where but a few seconds before there was joy, gaiety, marketing and peace, at the sound of the words: "The Wasambye," there was emptiness.

November 23rd:

Halt at mouth of Ruiki River.

We made a little progress in making friends with the Wagenya but the people were so timid that it required great tact to purchase one day's food and I really think that what they sold to us was but for the sake of not exasperating us, to satisfy ourselves, while they should remove their property to some of the islands opposite.

We rested all day here, hoping to hear some news of the land party, but though we made two expeditions up the Ruiki to hunt out news of them, night came leaving us regretting that we had divided the Expedition.

November 24th:

Sent Manwa Sera and 5 men up the river to hunt up news of the land party, I proceeded 10 miles up the Ruiki . . . At night we returned and met those sent up who returned with news of the Expedition who were then camped north of Makula's—3 days wanderings to make 8 geographical miles. They had gone far to the north-west. One was attacked and had 2 spears thrown at him. The young fellows whom I sent to search the Expedition out were attacked by a large party who threw 4 spears at them. By running to the river and seizing a canoe they saved themselves.

[*See illustration facing page* 161]

November 25th:

Crossed the Ruiki R. with the Expedition. A little before it arrived, a tragedy took place. A foolish old man persisted in advancing to the canoes to repossess himself of one, and being repeatedly driven off by main force, finally advancing with a spear and cheered by a mob on the other side of the Ruiki, one of my boy gun-bearers lifted up a rifle and shot him in the heart. I unfortunately was absent, having gone up the Lualaba to meet the Expedition, or I might have saved the foolish but determined old man.

November 26th:

Floated down Lualaba to Makanpemba. Overland march 14 miles.

Natives are so wild here they will not stay to be questioned, they are only to be captured by stratagem and made friends by force. We to sustain ourselves are obliged to make free with what they leave behind, which sometimes is very little, in other places abundant enough. At one place we obtained 15 goats which though insufficient to feed a force of 458 men was considered a satisfactory sop. Roasting ears of Indian corn and *manioc* [*tapioca*] plucked up, made up our very homely diet. Another man was shot uselessly enough I thought, and gave strictest orders that no native should be molested unless he was near camp at night. During the day they were permitted to come and go as they pleased. This fearful dread of the Wangwana or Wasambye has been taught them by the land pirate and heartless kidnapper Mtagomoyo or Muini Mubara.

November 27th:

Floated down Lualaba about 4 miles, came to place near Lukassa Rapids.

Natives extremely insolent, had a brush, two natives killed. West end of hilly ridge seen from Nakanpemba. We came to rapids and falls, steered close inshore and made all fast.

With 10 men I started down the left bank to explore, leaving orders for Frank Pocock and men not to stir until my return. In the woods found natives preparing ambuscades below the second rapids, some of the oldest directing some of the younger warriors where to conceal themselves. Canoes were also being hidden in a small cove with paddles near by. We found all this out on first hearing voices and concealing ourselves, and their manoeuvres were plainly revealed. A mile lower down were a

141

fleet of about 50 canoes, engaged in shifting things from the main land to the island on whose either side several rapids were. We opened the ball, and soon ousted the ambuscade, and some sheep were seized as spoil of the victors. We also made the island too hot to hold them, as in our operations of clearing the several rapids it was most undesirable to have an enemy lurking in the grass or reeds below the rapids.

On returning from the rendezvous, I was alarmed on hearing that Frank Pocock had permitted four of my best men to shoot the rapids in canoes, upon which I nothing doubted some calamity, as we had witnessed the hostile manoeuvres of the natives. After sending ten men down left bank, I was rejoiced to hear the men though chased had escaped, but regretted to hear that three Snyders were lost. The foolish people had shot two rapids, but at the third were upset and only one of the four managed to save his rifle. They had been swept into a whirlpool, sucked in, taken to the bottom, and shot to the surface some feet below the pool. Sitting astride of their canoes they were chased by the natives, but one revolver and rifle saved them. They paddled to land with their hands and were soon discovered and rescued by the land party.

Tonight we are camped below the first rapids on the left bank with noise of falling and rushing water all around us.

November 26th:

Halt.

Today I commenced work by floating the canoes down two rapids all successful. Then manned 4 canoes and boat and proceeded down river about 6 miles to see if there were any more falls. Though the river was exceedingly swift in some places owing to its extreme shallowness and narrowness not above 600 yards wide, there were no falls . . .

Stanley continued to float down the Lualaba River making about 4 miles a day, and although by December 5th the land party had still not caught up with him, he was not unduly alarmed since the land party consisted of 350 souls with 120 guns to defend them.

December 6th:

Halt at Ikondu.

Went down Lualaba 2 miles on right bank to explore. Came to a large party of natives 400–500 gathered on bank. They were fiercely demonstrative, but as we were only 8 in number we spoke them fair and patiently vowed we came on peaceful duty. We were answered with a flight of arrows to which we replied deliberately with Snyders and killed 3 and wounded several more, while we suffered no loss, and returned to camp . . .

In the afternoon after we had been long amused with the various sounds of horn-blowing on the opposite side, 8 large canoes were seen slowly making headway across the current on the opposite side, which finally came to the north point of Masuku Island, when they shouted out to us to meet them. We accepted the challenge, went out to meet them with the boat and one canoe carrying 20 guns. As we approached, we opened on them with the elephant rifle, two shots planted right amongst them. Two men leapt into the water, one sank immediately, the other not surrendering was despatched. Some more successful shots created panic amongst them and sent them flying down river. Meantime seven other canoes loaded with perhaps a hundred men which had approached Ikondu along the left bank, seeing the flight of their confederates along the right bank, returned with inglorious speed . . .

On December 11*th Stanley discovered that the land party was severely infected with smallpox. By December* 13*th, smallpox was raging throughout the united camp, 6 people had died and about* 30 *were sick.*

December 14*th:*

Float down Lualaba River 5 miles.

Mutako natives made a first class plan of attack, two sides by water, one side by land, but it failed from their want of courage. One canoe sufficed to drive the water party, and 2 guns the land party.

December 15*th:*

Halt to obtain food.

Tippu-Tib's concubine died of smallpox, the 8th victim since the 11th instant.

December 18th:

We came from Kisui Kachiambi to Kisunga's market place. Halted a short while to enable land party to reach us. Not coming, sent a small party west to hunt up news of them. This party arrived before a village where spears were thrown at them, and in turn they made a clean sweep of the village and captured a woman and child which they brought to me. By means of these captives I succeeded in checking the demonstrativeness of the Mpika Island people and inducing them to refrain from indulging in war. We made peace and brotherhood with them, and the news spread quickly, and we heard shouts of "Go in peace." Then descending the river we came to Vinya-Njara where we made preparations to camp. After clearing out a landing place, the people began to stir about to prepare food. While digging peanuts, a shower of arrows continued until night and the next morning the arrows fell, when, perceiving we had sufficient cause to begin war, we made a stockade, built three stockades on three ant hills commanding the village, sent out scouts to the forest . . . At noon I went in a canoe to get the latitude and by means of field glasses discovered the nest whence the arrows came; descending a short distance until I came within range, I took aim and succeeded in dropping a Chief . . .

December 20th:

Halt.

Made a night expedition and captured 4 canoes. Sent a land expedition to search for the enemy, wounded one man. I killed one yesterday who was probably a Chief or an influential person for the weeping and sorrow was great and since then they have become utterly unnerved.

The savages were not the only ones; Tippu-Tib and his men were so unnerved and determined to retrace their steps to Nyangwe that Stanley saw no choice but to release the Arabs and Wanyamwezi from their contract and continue downstream with his own loyal followers.

December 25th:

Halt.

December 1876

Christmas Day. Passed orderly and quietly with a certain amount of cheerfulness inspired by the hope that before many months we shall reach the sea.

Foot races between young and old were inaugurated to our great amusement.

December 27th:

Halt.

We are prepared to go tomorrow for good. Tippu-Tib for his services has received a draft for $2,600. After we are gone he waits about two days and starts for Kima-Kima on the Rumami River about West by North from here.

The Wanyamwezi gave us a farewell dance, excellently well done. I thought it would be very fine and cheering if our people could sing and dance so well.

To Tippu-Tib I gave 1 silver goblet, 1 wooden box, 1 gold chain, 30 *doti* cloth, 2 *fras:* beads, 6,300 shells, 1 pistol, 200 ammunition, 2 coils brass wire.

On December 28th the Expedition waved goodbye to Tippu-Tib and the Wanyamwezi and rowed away down-river. No longer having to halt every other day to allow the land party to catch up, the Expedition, now fully water-borne with purchased canoes, was able to make better progress, although it was thenceforth entirely responsible for its own defence.

December 30th:

We made but 4 miles today owing to rainy weather and a storm. The morning was passed on the shore of Luru or Lulu where natives of Iryamba made friends with us and sold us a few bananas and palm butter. At about 2 p.m. in the afternoon the rain having ceased, we pulled across to Iryamba when a storm arose in the crossing and two heavily loaded river canoes sank; two men were drowned . . . and 4 guns were lost, which makes 7 guns lost in this river.

I feared this disaster would cause the people to rebel and return, but I was cheered to hear that they deemed it nothing more than Fate, and if Fate had ordained that we should perish, to return or proceed would present no escape. It was therefore better to go on, said the Chiefs. We have had omens and

145

sayings plentiful enough to forbid our further progress, but down-river has such charm that we are compelled to go on. I hope to God there are no tremendous cataracts ahead; with steep hills on each side of the river, such a place would indeed be a chasm.

December 31st:

Continue the journey down river to uninhabited island 182 geographical miles North $\frac{1}{2}$ East from Nyangwe.

Journey today though not long was prosperous, the day fine. Island near the Iryamba, north, very populous and large, natives belligerent. Made tactics for a naval fight but changed their minds prudently and retired without exchange of hurtful salutes. I find it terrible trouble to take charge of so many people totally innocent of anything approaching to manliness or sense on water. It is one protracted torture, chest aches with violent shouting and upbraiding them for their foolish cowardice, voice becomes hoarse with giving orders which in a few seconds are entirely forgotten.

I have 143 souls, men, women and children, 2 riding asses, 2 goats and 1 sheep.

> Out of these 143, 107 are enlisted men in my employ for wages.
> Out of these 107 only 48 have guns.
> Out of these 48 only 32 are effective men who would be able to make a tolerable resistance.
> Add to these 32 men, myself and Frank Pocock, and we are 34 fighting men, 109 are mere dummies which serve to frighten off savages deterred by a show of heads rather than arms.

They are terribly dull people to lead across Africa. They smoke *banghy* until they literally fall down half smothered. It took me nearly 2 years to teach my boatmen how to row a boat and to take charge of her. After 2 years practice, one fellow, Muscati, loaded his gun with paper and a bullet and was surprised that his gun did not fire. On nearing an island, I shouted out to one of my boatmen, Rojab, to seize the branches of a tree to prevent us being swept from the landing by the current. "Yes, sir," he shouted, and jumped on land and seized the bushes; while the boat was swept away leaving him on the island. At one landing I shouted, when about to continue our journey, to push away. Muscati stood in his canoe, bent his back double, seized his canoe pushing away manfully and was surprised when his canoe did not budge. Muini Hassan, Captain of a canoe, being told to punt his canoe up into a creek, called one of his crew to assist him. His man punted all right, but the Captain braced his pole forward against his man, and finding his canoe was obstinate, scolded his man heartily for about 5 minutes, who had to continue against the strong current and the Captain's punting pole.

January 1st, 1877:

Continue the journey from uninhabited island to Kerembuka. The journey was mostly through uninhabited forests, except that there was one large settlement on island and mainland. Until today we were called Wasambye. We were today called Wajiwa and our guns called *katadzi* while before they were called *kibongeh* or lightning. We were gliding gently down past the settlement and attempting in mild tones to make pacific overtures, addressed as Friends, and greeted them with the word *Sen-nen-neh* or "Peace". We got no answer though we saw them plainly enough behind the plantains and trees, crouching with drawn bows. We passed them by. Then our gentle and quiet behaviour was regarded by them as cowardice, and their wooden war drums were beaten and immediately 14 canoes well manned dashed out from the creeks and the island, others following in full chase after us, loaded with shouting crews, and with them broad shields—door-like. I at once anchored in midstream, while the canoes took shelter along an islet sheltered by overhanging mangrove. I waited some time to allow the natives to advance. They floated down to 300 yards of the boat and halted their canoes on the mainland. I aimed at the nearmost canoe and fortunately struck two with the first bullet, at the sight of which they all precipitated themselves into the water and cried out: "Let them go, before we are all exterminated. These people will not be stopped. Let them go, we are dead." Before this they were saying: "We shall eat Wajiwa today."

Such fools it is hardly possible to imagine as these. At one place, Ikondu, they set nets to catch us, and one was shot in the act of setting a large game net. They considered us as game to be trapped, shot, or bagged at sight.

January 2nd:

Continue the journey down river to Katumbi.

Today has been a lively day with us. At Lombo-a-Kiriro, we made friends, and permitted 4 large canoes, one about 90 feet long manned with 35 paddlers, to pass by with a peaceful salutation. After giving the word "Peace", and going down a little, we saw we were followed by them and others coming from Kibombo Island and Amu Nyam. It seemed to me we were about to have a busy time. I did not wait to be surrounded, but at once dropped anchor and opened fire, while the canoes were sent ashore to do damage. The people seeing we were not to be victims as they had intended, ran away, and we seized eatables and canoes and captured 2 women. One we have released to carry a message of peace to her friends, with a promise that if they make peace we shall release the other, as we are not come for war but to see the river. At Katumbi about dusk a native was seen thrusting a spear into the camp. About 6 natives fell today in the passage down river.

January 3rd:

Continue journey from Katumbi down Rowwa River to Baswa Banki Rapids.

We began the journey pleasantly enough. About 3 miles below Katumbi we came to a great number of low islands, separated from the right bank by a narrow stream which we descended. We soon came to a number of canoes, some dozen in number, whose crews were terribly frightened. Greeting them peacefully they loudly responded to our cry of peace, and we passed on followed by several of them who received permission to indulge their curiosity. For three hours our descent was not marred, and we hoped that a day so auspiciously begun would end so, but at Mwana-Ntaba where we left a boy and a woman in a canoe loaded with food to pass unmolested, our pleasure was soon turned to war. Drums, horns, cries along the banks summoned the people to arms, who presently appeared with shields and spears to interrupt our descent.

For two hours we fought with them at the end of which, finding they had retired, we continued our descent as far as the Mikonju River. Mwana-Ntaba ends at the south bank of the Mikonju and the country of the Baswa tribe begins who soon manifested their aversion to strangers by challenging us and coming up from the islands in the Rapids to us. On rounding the point at the north bank of the Mikonju we soon saw the reason of their ferocity in the Rapids, which was an obstacle to delay us and to give them an opportunity to test our prowess and courage. We accepted the challenge after peace was refused, and a few rounds sent them flying. Near the Rapids on the right bank we constructed a strong camp. Elephants very numerous by recent tracks. Slept undisturbed save by shrill weird cries of the lemur and gorilla.

January 4th:

Baswa Rapids [*re-named the First Cataract of the Stanley Falls*].
While engaged in making several coils of rope out of the lianes or convolvuli we were disturbed again by the Baswa who were again repelled, while each successful shot was responded to with wild cries of surprise, rage, and sorrow mixed. A small party was sent to survey the right bank below, but the whole force of the river almost rushed with intense impetuosity against the right bank which formed a deep bend, barring all possibility of proceeding by the right branch and numerous wrecks of canoes strewed along shore testified to the destructive force of the waters. I then manned 2 double canoes and crossed above the Rapids to the left bank along which ran a small stream though deep and but little disturbed, which presently broke into numerous foamy streams among rocky islands covered with mangrove, others with palms, bananas, and fields of the fierce Baswa tribe. One small branch still continued its quiet flow but presently this fell also rapidly over sheets of dark brown rock.

January 5th:

Crossed over to the left bank and descended by the left branch and camped near its Falls. Having discovered that to float the canoes down the Falls was impossible, I sent the men to work to cut a road 20 feet wide through the dense jungle. A mile in length was found sufficient to take us below the Falls to where the stream renewed its quiet flow. Within this mile there are two Falls of about 4 feet and two steep rapids down which the water rushes with terrible force. Owing to the severe punishment given to the Baswa 2 days previously, we were not disturbed today in our work. Tomorrow we hope to begin dragging the canoes overland below the Falls.

January 6th:

Commenced the work of hauling the canoes by land below the Falls. By noon we had carried the boat, and dragged seven canoes. A furious rain then set in which put a stop to the work. Our force is now divided a half below the Falls and half above. The Baswa having been quieted have abandoned the attempt to molest us.

January 7th:

This morning continued our labours, and by noon we were all embarked in our canoes and afloat once more. Descended cautiously about 4 miles along the left bank, and landed at Cheandoah Island of the Baswa tribe who had challenged us to war. Landed a force and captured the Island after three shots! The suddenness of our arrival had completely upset their calculations and their spirit. We captured about 30 goats and had an abundance of food, bananas, chickens, eggs with an immense amount of native African booty consisting of spears, knives, shields, iron wire etc. We also captured a woman and child to whom we were indebted for names of places and other local information, amongst which we heard of a terrible tribe called the Bakumu Cannibals who make a clean sweep of tribes such as the Wavinza, Mwana-Ntaba and Baswa. They are armed with bows and arrows. We are told also that they have heard of us and mean to see of what stuff we are made.

January 8th:

Halt at Cheandoah Island.
Explored island, found it defended on each side by terrible Falls and Rapids. Explored right bank found no road, then

150

crossed over to left bank which to our minds seemed easier. Captured a man today who repaid us with lies. He was perfectly unintelligible to all our interpreters.

West of the island, Cheandoah presents a picture of the force of a large river descending a steep slope. Enormous whirlpools with the centre about 18 inches below the edge. We pushed an empty canoe into the influence of one, saw it whirled round, drawn in, and shot up again stern foremost. Another singular scene I witnessed: in the neighbourhood of the Rapids are circular basins of rock and still streamlike reaches of water, which every now and then are strongly agitated, rise nearly a foot immediately and as quickly subside.

January 9th:

Left Cheandoah Island and crossed over to left bank. As we were exploring a creek that seemed to follow a course of the river, we were surprised to see a large crowd of natives in war paint and with shields. No work could be done in the jungle, such as road-making, with camps undefended, if they were permitted to overawe the working parties or to wound one single man. These were the terrible Bakumu, who had made mincemeat of so many tribes, and who have promised to try our mettle. The boat came out of the creek and a single shot cleared the banks while loud cries of women and shouts of men testified to its success. We then landed and guided by the cries followed them, and came to two villages strongly defended with heaped brushwood and prostrated trees, where we found the people prepared for a fight. Charging through the bush we entered the first village and drove them flying into the woods with a loss of five or six more. About 60 shields and a 100 spears were found thrown away by the fugitives. We then set fire to the villages and retraced our steps to begin the work of cutting out a road, and hauling the canoes overland. By night we had cut our road and dragged all our canoes on land . . .

January 10th:

Completed the work of hauling the canoes from Bakumu villages on left bank to river north of Cheandoah and opposite Ntunduru Island. Made our camp on a small island protected by a fosse-like stream, and cut a road 1½ miles long to to-morrow's camp.

January 11th:

Floated the canoes down two miles of stream and Rapids to camp opposite north end of Ntunduru Island. It has been a terribly trying day. Six canoes were floated down safely enough early in the morning. The seventh canoe was taken by Muscati, Uledi Muscati and Zaidi, one of my Captains. Muscati, the steersman, did not understand his work and soon upset his canoe in a piece of bad rapids which soon smashed it to pieces. Muscati and Uledi managed to swim to Ntunduru where they were shortly after saved by the Chief Captain Manwa Sera, but poor Zaidi was slightly [*stunned?*] by the roar of waters and unfortunately clung to a piece of the canoe which was swept by our camp in full view with frightful speed to what seemed inevitable death. Providence, however, interposed to save him even on the brink of Eternity. The great Falls at the north end of Ntunduru Island was split by a single pointed rock, on which the fragment of canoe was driven, the lower end got jammed below, and Zaidi found himself perched in the centre of the Falls, with about 50 yards of falling water and furious black-brown waves on either side of him.

Called to the scene, I could scarcely believe my eyes or realise what strange chance had placed him there, and a more aweful scene I could hardly believe few men had witnessed than I did. The solitary man seated on the pointed rock with the brown waves rising up to his knees seemed to be much calmer than any of us who gazed upon him in his terrible position. We then cast about for means to save him. We first lashed several lengths of creepers to a canoe and lowered it down to him, but the instant it seemed to reach him, the force of the running water was so great that the stout creeper snapped like pack thread and the canoe swept by like an arrow, and was engulfed. Then we tried to toss sticks, stools—wooden—into the middle of the stream, but everything was swept away and still the silent man sat witnessing our repeated efforts and we felt each moment that his doom was certain though protracted.

Then I called for another canoe and to this I lashed an inch rope—tent rope—and two stout creepers each 70 yards long and got two volunteers to enter the canoe and paddle it to mid-stream, which of itself was hard work. Five times this method failed to reach him; the sixth time getting more emboldened as the rope and creepers proved strong, we managed to touch his arm, but the current swept it away immediately. The seventh time Zaidi was struck by the creeper thrown to him and instantly fell like a shot into the gulf below. Thirty seconds passed and as no signs of him were seen, we feared he was lost and began to look for his struggling form in the waves below, when his head rose slowly above the waters. "Pull away", I shouted, tent rope and the two creepers parted, and the canoe began to move down the opposite Falls, but Zaidi acting like an anchor caused the canoe to veer to an island below the Falls and all three working as desperate men can work managed to bring the canoe to the island all safe. Though we hurrahed with relieved hearts, their position was still but a reprieve from death. A Fall 50 yards in width separated the island from us, and to the right was a Fall about 300 yards wide, and below them was half a mile of Falls and Rapids and great whirlpools and waves rising like hills in the middle of the terrible stream, and below these were the cannibals of Wane-Mukwa. How to reach the island was the question which now perplexed us. We tied a stone to about 60 yards of whipcord and after about the 50th effort they managed to catch it. To the end of the whipcord they tied the tent rope, which had parted before, and drawing it to our side, tied it to three stout creepers, which they drew across and fastened to a rock, by which we thought we had bridged the stream. "Now the boldest of you pull yourself across." We heard them debating as to who should go first. Then Uledi, one of the volunteers, shouting: "In the name of God," climbed gallantly into the stream, but alas he had made but two pulls when the faithless convolvuli broke and he was compelled to pull back to the island, where as night had now fallen we left them after many encouragements and returned to our camp.

Meantime, the eighth canoe, whose steersman was the coxswain of the *Lady Alice,* had likewise got upset, and the coxswain out of six who were upset was drowned to my great regret as my boat-people were the most select out of the Expedition for smartness, civility, bravery, and every other quality which endears a follower to a Commander. Heavens! An awful day altogether, not very unlike January 12th, 1876.

January 12th, 1877:

My first duty this morning was to send greetings to my three brave boys on the Island in the Falls and to send assurances that preparations were being made for their deliverance. I set a party of 30 men to search for strong cane and another to make communications again with whipcord with the island. About 9 a.m. abundance of 2 inch cane, 1 inch and $\frac{1}{2}$ inch were brought with which we prepared three lines, each sufficient to sustain three men in the water, but to make assurance and success trebly sure, we succeeded in sending three lines across to the island which they fastened to the rocky points. Then hailing them, I asked them if they were sure they could haul themselves across; if not, I would send each man a separate line to tie round his waist. They shouted a reply that if I was sure the lines would not break, they could; to which I answered that they would haul a ship across. Then Uledi lifted his hands up, muttered a short prayer and laughingly leapt in, catching hold of the cables as he fell into the depths of the Falls. Soon he rose, hauling himself hand over hand, the waves brushing his face and rising over his head, until it seemed as if he could never find time to breath, but by jerking his body upward occasionally with a desperate effort, he so managed as to survive the waves and to haul himself across near to us, where a score of hands stood ready to snatch the half smothered man. Zaidi next followed but, after the tremendous proof he gave of his courage and deliberately tenacious hold, not much fear was entertained for him and he came safe to be congratulated for his double escape from death.

Marzouk, the youngest, was the last and we held our very breaths while the gallant boy struggled with the terrible rush of water. In the middle of raising himself to breathe, he let go of two lines and barely caught hold of the third, and our anxiety was intense for a few seconds lest he should despair and relax his hold; and to prevent this I shouted out harshly: "Pull away, you fool. Be a man." At which with three strokes he pulled himself within reach of our willing hands to be hugged and fondled by all. The cheers we gave were heard far above the roar of the waters, and the camp heard it and knew that the three most gallant lads of the Expedition had been saved.

When we had collected ourselves a little, we set to work to begin cutting the road 1½ miles long to pass this terrible scene altogether by land.

At the north end of Ntunduru, four separate streams unite in so many Falls and Rapids and then the limited waters gather themselves into one huge boiling cauldron, and a mound-like body of water, and hurls itself down several feet with tremendous uproar just south of Asama Island. The distance is barely ¾ mile but it is one of the wildest sights of raging waters, brown waves et cetera conceivable . . .

January 13*th:*

Halt in camp opposite Ntunduru Island.

Men engaged in hauling canoes over land, a distance of 2 miles. I went ahead with my boat boys to explore ahead and to resolve how much longer extend these Falls. By night we had hauled the canoes 1 mile.

The minute hot-water ants that infest these jungles are a great annoyance. The men's backs are covered with great blisters, while my scalp smarts as if wounded with a fine steel comb. I have had several times occasion to bless myself that our single victory over the savage Bakumu has left us unmolested in our terrible work.

January 14*th:*

Hauled our canoes over the remaining mile of land into the river below the Great Falls between Asama and Ntunduru, but we have another Fall about a mile below, opposite the south end of Asama Island.

January 15*th:*

Cut road along river to lower canoes down stream by hand, to Lower Falls. Also road across to below Falls. The Asama islanders have challenged us to fight.

January 16*th:*

Thank God we are camped tonight below the Lowest Falls

of this long series and are halting tonight at the point opposite the south end of Asama Island.

January 17th:

Crossed over early this morning to Asama Island and literally took possession. Abundance of food to pay us for our long sojourn in the wilderness.

The river journey continued, Stanley pausing to investigate a curious cavern of pisolitic limestone *and to note that the* natives of Kipanga Island and Asama, hearing dreadful reports of us hung their charms, feathers and leaves across the landing places, which we interpreted as not at home.

They continued down stream at the rate of about 1½ *miles a day, negotiating Falls and Rapids until January 23rd when a halt was made* to repair boat which has become deranged somewhat from her rough journey over rocks.

January 26th:

Descended one mile to the Wenya Falls and cut a road across a neck of land beyond which is the Wenya Creek on the right bank . . . Fall is about 10 feet but there is a great slope and as the river narrows to about 500 yards, the force of the current is terrific, as it rushes through the narrows to the grand breadth below Wenya Island.

These Wenya [*Wagenya?*] are cunning and skilful people in some things, but their villages are untidy. They are clever at wooden boxes, paddles, cord making.

Ivory seems to be a drug with them. Three large tusks I found to be perfectly rotten in the villages. They seem to have no use for it after cutting off a foot off the point for the purpose of making war horns and pestles to pound corn,

They catch an enormous amount of fish by means of the poles and conical baskets attached to long canes.

It was here, where the River turned decisively westward, that a city was to rise named after the Explorer himself—Stanleyville.

January 27th:

Descended over 200 yards of rocks by a system of railway sleepers topped with rollers, and then 2 miles of a series of waterfalls and rapids which this creek makes until it approaches the north end of Wenya Island, when it becomes still and sluggish.

The Wenya planned to attack us by two points, one from the north end of Wenya Island ascending up-creek and the other by striking right across River to take us in rear while our working parties were scattered over a length of two miles dragging heavy canoes over the rock terraces. Thirteen guns and a few successful well placed shots sent them flying to the village at the point opposite Wenya Island on the right bank.

January 29th:

Voyage continues from Usimbi to Erere Island.

Today we have had three fights. Obliged to fight by the savage insolence of men and women. The men generally ranged themselves on the banks with shields and spears, shouting their war cries. To have passed them by in silence would have been to invite further molestation. We at once landed and punished them several times. In the last fight opposite this night's camp Muftah Rufigi of the Mgindo was killed by a desperate savage who attacked him with a knife 18 inches long which cut him on the head, almost severed the right arm from the shoulder, and then was buried up to the hilt in his chest.

January 30th:

Voyage continues from Erere Island to uninhabited island 6 miles north-west by west from Yangambi.

We were assaulted in the most determined manner by the natives of populous Yangambi. They were in full war paint, and all the medicines and charms were brought forth. They were the bravest we met. Of course, such arrogance met with instant punishment. In an instant we had landed spearmen and musketeers, and in their rear fire was set to the village. We then withdrew to a grassy islet to observe the effect on the natives, lunched, and as they had drawn together on the banks, made a second attempt. But the fire and their losses in dead had quelled their courage. We then proceeded on our way down river, passed two abandoned settlements, the results of former wars . . .

January 31st:

Voyage continues from Divari Island.

Today I thought I would try to pass one day without fighting, but just as we left Divari Island we rounded a point where amplest preparations had been made. They had been up all night with drums, building a palisade, making charms, etc. Uganza and Irende opposite had also come up with canoes which they had hidden behind our little island to demonstrate when opportunity offered to our disadvantage. We therefore floated quietly down by them, probably without a shot, had not a mischievous fellow rose up and swayed his spear. He was hushed with one shot, and no more was attempted. We then thought it would be advisable to steer close to the islands and look resolutely away from the natives, but after passing Mawembe some distance, we were followed by six or seven canoes who pulled lustily after us and called out to others hidden behind the small island to advance and eat us. A few harmless shots allayed their rage for our flesh and we came down peacefully to camp on an uninhabited island 17 miles north-west of Mawembe.

The utmost vigilance is necessary each night to prevent theft of canoes and night surprises, for the natives are very capable of it. By day, also, for the islands are numerous and communications of alarm and war combinations rapid enough to excite admiration, by means of their enormous wooden drums which are heard at a great distance.

February 1st:

Voyage continues from camp on uninhabited island.

Today has been another busy day, had three fights, in which the natives must have lost about 30 lives. They first sought to attack us at a market place as we passed by, but we sharply turned round, landed, killed about 10, got an abundance of food and then set fire to the canoes—about 25 in number. At a second market place a similar scene took place. Then proceeded from noon to about 3 p.m. We came to Battle River [*River Aruwimi*]. Twenty-three canoes came from the left bank. Twenty-one canoes came from Battle River, about 10 of which were enormous things containing probably about 500 men. They advanced to the attack bravely enough with drums and horns and cries. We in the meantime dropped anchor and arranged ourselves in a line across the stream which ran between the mainland and an island at the mouth of Battle River. In a short time we had given them a taste of what they might expect from us, and caused some of the largest to retire wailing. Some of their men were in the river, others lay in the bottom of the canoes groaning and dying. As these retired, a magnificent war canoe came down to reinforce them. It probably was the King's canoe, and contained about 100 men. About 6 were perched on a platform at the bow, hideously painted and garnished with head-dresses of feathers, while one stalked backwards and forwards with a crown of feathers. There were probably about 60 paddlers and each paddle was decorated with an ivory ball handle and the staff was wound about with copper and iron wire.

In the next 2 days the Expedition travelled 9 miles into the territory of Bemberri.

February 3rd:

Land lies very low, islands so numerous that it is impossible to note more than appears near our line of downward progress. The natives are so savage that we are compelled for the sake of avoiding wars to sneak among the islands, all of which are uninhabited. The river is now from 5–8 miles wide.

The natives of Bemberri would not permit us to pass by peacefully. To our cries that we had no cause for war, that we were peaceful, they replied with stones and swaying of spear, drumming and noise. The racket they made with their enormous wooden drums was perfectly terrific; though it did not disturb us much, except our ears, it inspired even their boys to exhibitions of ferocious valour.

We endeavoured to do our best to avoid a conflict with the savages and happily succeeded, though at noon it was extremely doubtful, for the Barundu sighted us as we passed the islands opposite and instantly manned 18 large canoes. They followed us for 10 miles or so and then it seems returned, for as we neared another country, we saw no more of them.

Livingstone called floating down the Lualaba a foolhardy feat. So it is, and were I to do it again, I would not attempt [*it*] without 200 guns. The natives, besides being savage, ferocious to an extreme degree, are powerful and have means by land and water to exercise to great lengths their ferocity. I pen these lines with half a feeling that they will never be read by any other white person; still as I persist in continuing the journey, I persist in writing, leaving events and their disposal to an All-Wise Providence. If we shall suffer on this journey, we suffer for the injuries done to the tribes above by Mtagamoyo and his confederates, for they have made the name of the Wasambye synonymous with robbers and pirates.

Day and night we are pained with the dreadful drumming which announces our arrival and their fears of our purposes. We have no interpreter, and cannot make ourselves understood.

Either bank is equally powerful, to go from one side to the other is like jumping from the frying pan into the fire. It may be said truly that we are now "Running the gauntlet".

February 7th:

[*Rubunga.*] River called Ikuta Yacongo.

Thank God. An anxious day has terminated with tranquillity to a long disturbed mind. Twenty-six fights on this river have reduced my ammunition so low, and we were still so far from the coast, that I began to fear we should find ourselves hemmed by savage enemies without means of resistance.

We floated down the river from 6.30 a.m. to 11 a.m. among the islands, having previously solemnly addressed the men, told them we had no food; if natives would not sell, we should have to take it by force, or storming. Each gun, spear, and even knife was therefore made ready. At 11 a.m. we sighted the village of Rubunga. Floated steadily towards it. Three canoes came to meet us without the usual savage demonstrations. We welcomed this as a good sign but not understanding what they said, they ran away and shields and spears presently bristled along the banks. Arriving near, dropped anchor, showed copper rings, brass wire, red beads, shells. They were baits, but what suspense, how slow to bite at them. What patience! Men clamoured for food; Prudence whispered Patience. Natives were slow to adopt peace. We showed bananas and drew in our stomachs to illustrate their emptiness.

H. M. Stanley with Kalulu. A photograph taken before the expedition left.

Photograph : Richard Stanley

A page from the author's field notebook.

returned with news of the Expedition who were
then Canoes North of Makula's three days
wandering, to make eight geographical miles.
They had gone far to the N.W. one was attacked
and had ten spears thrown at him. The young
fellows whom I sent to search the Exped-out were
attacked by a large party who threw four spears
at them. By running to the river & seizing a canoe
they saved themselves.

Some of the Waganya huts are decorated
round with human teeth driven in like nails
around the edge.

Nov. 25th Crossed the Ruiki R. with the Expedition. A little before it arrived a tragedy took
place. A foolish old man persisted in danc-
ing to the canoes to repossess himself of one
and being repeatedly driven off by main force
finally advancing with a spear & cheered by
a mob on the other side of the Ruiki, one
of my boy gunbearers lifted up a rifle &
shot him in the heart. I unfortunately was
absent having gone up the Inalaba to shell
the Expedition, or I might have saved the foolish
but determined old man.

Kasongo
Ukanda
Makura's
Kalabo

Sketch of Bridge Island from the author's notebook.

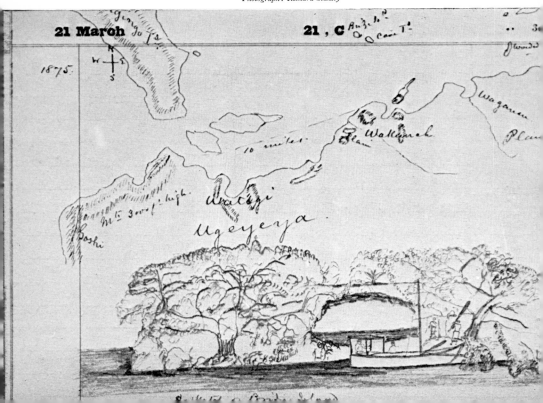

21 March
21, C
1875.
10 miles
Mts 3000ft high
Urarigi
Ugeyeya
Poshi
Wakignah
Waganu
Plain

Finally, they made signs for us to go to a small island opposite and they would bring us food. We went and we waited a couple of hours. We saw them packing goats, bananas, food, such things as we looked at with greedy eyes, in their canoes and paddling with them down river. Our men eyed them solemnly and murmured: "You see what fools we are to put trust in a heathen's word. The cunning devils only wanted us to give them time to hide their things. When we do assault the place, as we must do, there will be but little left to satisfy hunger."

"Well, my men," I said, "wait a little and if they do not come to us we will go to them and eat them."

At 1 p.m. we crossed over, savage at heart and desperately hungry, most of the men with the resolve to waste no words but to shoot and take the place and forage at will. The boat led the way as usual, but I saw the natives so clearly, they presented such easy targets that a blind man might have shot a dozen, that I relented, thinking it a pity to shoot people who took no pains to conceal themselves. Besides, their conduct, though somewhat distrustful was not to be compared with the arrogant savages we had run the gauntlet lately.

I told them in a mixture of Kiswahili, Kikusu and Kibaswa, that if they did not bring food, I must take it or we would die. They must sell it for beads, red, blue, or green, copper or brass wire or shells, or. . . . I drew significant signs across the throat. It was enough, they understood at once, and we hailed it heartily. To confirm their understanding, I threw them ashore a copper bracelet and a string of shells. They clapped hands, laughed, we hurrahed, made blood brotherhood, before we steered from the anchorage before the village and peace was concluded.

These natives outdo all I have seen for tattooing.

February 8th:

Halt at Rubunga in Nganza.

Early this morning, trade, a certain sign of peace began, and lasted without any unpleasant interruption until night. For the first time for many weeks we enjoyed that calmness of mind which is only enjoyed by the happy few who know neither care nor anxiety. A hearty geniality pervaded the market island. Hundreds of canoes, light swift things, came from

many parts . . . Food was cheap and abundant: cassava, fresh
and dried fish, dog meat, live dogs and goats, bananas, robes of
grass cloth, spears, knives, axes, bells, iron bracelets and girdles,
in fact every mortal thing known in Africa was saleable and
purchasable.

February 9th:

Voyage continues from Rubunga in Nganza to Urangi.

Tsetse and gad-fly are most numerous on the river, biting
men and animals with a voracity unseen hitherto.

My mind is mostly employed in creating imaginary difficulties and in finding how to overcome them.

February 10th:

Descend the river for about 2 hours to Urangi, a large town
about a mile long erected close to the river on a low bank.
Welcomed at Urangi because our liberality at Rubunga had
made us many friends.

February 11th:

Voyage continues.

In writing my notes of yesterday, I said we were welcomed
at Urangi. At first so we were, but at about 3 p.m. our people
had to complain of many things stolen. One had his mat and
cloth, other lost his axe, another a couple of spears, and we
were finally obliged to drive them out of camp and to build a
boma. Still trade went on in the canoes cheerily enough, though
a little less noise was noticeable. Blood brotherhoods had also
been made and a dance on our part concluded a peaceful day.

Early this morning we set out from our camp opposite
Urangi preceded by two guides to introduce us to Ukataraka
two days below, and the down voyage began and lasted just
10 minutes smooth and agreeable. Suddenly I heard a gunshot
from Manwa Sera's canoe and our people cried out: "They are
throwing spears."

Our guides deserted us instantly, and in rising in the boat
to take a view of my surroundings, I found that about 30 canoes
starting out from the village before us, and about 50 from
Urangi coming behind us, was too much of a prearrangement
not to conclude at once that the natives did not intend to permit

us to depart without trying our mettle. The boat dropped behind to form a line of battle. Our canoes were formed in line and ordered to pull steadily down river. The boat formed rearguard and opened on the natives with Snyders which soon cleared the river with great loss to the savages. About four had their crews struggling in the water.

About 2 hours brought us to Mpakiwana, a very large village. These also came out, followed us with spears and war horns for 3 miles, until we opened fire on them, killed two or three and drove them back. We then continued our journey between the islands as before.

Manwa Sera, through carelessness or terror after his first shot, permitted his Snyder to fall into the river. This makes the 8th gun lost on the river, the 4th of which he is the cause. A fate follows us in our guns certainly, for out of 100 with which we left the coast, we have only 52 left.

February 13th:

Voyage continues.

We have all the pleasures as well as all the terrors of river life. We glide down narrow streams, between palmy and spicy islands, whose sweet fragrance and vernal colour cause us to forget for a moment our dangerous life. We have before us the winding shores of islands, crowned with eternal spring life and verdure. Teak and Cotton-wood, palms, Guinea and the Ware-Palm, the tall cane with its drooping feathery leaves, the bushy and many rooted Mangrove which flourishes by the water side, here and there a low grassy bank from which the crocodile plunges into the brown depths, the snorting and watchful Behemoth whose roar, echoed between tall banks of woods, has its volume redoubled. The terrors are rocks and rapids, the roaring plunging dreadful cataract, the sudden storms which wrinkle the river's face into a dangerous aspect, the savages which howled after us and required us for meat . . .

I had just penned the above, inspired to it by a slight sense of enjoyment, when lo! we came in sight of a village, and immediately war drums and horns sounded their defiance. As we approached, we lay on our oars and permitted some dozen large canoes loaded with menacing savages to wheel and paddle about, expecting every moment war to begin, for such a surly scowling set I have seldom seen. In response to our friendly greetings, they aimed at us with their muskets, and there were probably 60 or 70 muskets pointed at us at one time. We pulled quietly by, and we were followed by six canoes, containing probably about 80 men, who exercised themselves in blowing a sonorous war horn. We descended this way for 2 miles, when suddenly I heard a musket shot and then another, and as I turned my head, I saw shot skipping over water towards us. Of course we replied quick sharp and fatal, and [*they*] were driven back in a panic with three or four killed, while we, thank God, had not suffered a scratch. Not even a canoe had been struck . . .

February 14*th:*

Voyage continues.

The fight of fights occurred today. It lasted from noon until 5 p.m. on the river. Up to near noon, we had rowed quietly down, then we sighted a village—whether on the main or an island I cannot say—and immediately we were announced with war cries and war drums. I halted behind a small island near the village to take meridian altitude and then set off [76°.7'30"]. From that spot to the end of the district, a distance of 10 miles, we maintained a running fight between 54 canoes and us. In each canoe there were from 10–20 men, so that we had over 300 men opposed to us. No one was hurt on our side, but the savages suffered more severely than ever I supposed they were capable of bearing. But the truth must be told, some of them showed great courage and aptitude for war. Others again fired their guns at an enormous distance from us. The hostility which these people bear for us is most strange, for as soon as they see us, without a word being spoken on either side, they man their canoes and fire away at us as if we were lawful game. By 5 p.m. we had run the gauntlet. I should not omit to state that in the middle of the fight some of our people saw food on shore, landed and seized it, which was small though valuable spoil to us.

February 15*th:*

Voyage continues.

We rowed from 8 a.m. until near noon. Halted to obtain

altitude of sun. Then rowed to 3 p.m. Storm arose, lasted 1½ hours. Rowed thence to 6 p.m. No event today, except thank God quiet rowing.

Distance gone today about 18 miles. The number of mosquitoes last night sounded to our half awakened senses like the noise of advancing savages. Few slept, and continually was heard the flip flap of branches from the poor tormented soldiers.

February 18*th:*

For three days we have been permitted by the mercy of God to descend this great river uninterrupted by the savage clamour and ferocity. Winds for two days were a slight impediment and a cause for anxiety. Yesterday was a fine calm day, the river like a sheet of glass and we made good progress. We saw a trading canoe manned with 15 paddlers clothed in loincloths of Joho or red blanketing. We hailed them but they did not answer us. This sight makes me believe that the river below is pretty free of Cataracts or Falls, and it may be that there are no more than the Cataract of Sundi and the Falls of Yellala, otherwise I cannot account for the ascent of these trading canoes and such extensive possession of cloths and guns so far up this river.

Trading goods for this river seemed to be red blanketing, Madrassee cloth, prints, Sofi beads, white beads, shells, guns, powder, flintstones.

Since February 9th, we have been unable to purchase food, or indeed approach a settlement for any amicable purpose, the natives have been so hostile. Even fishing canoes have fired at us as though we were harmless game. God alone knows how we shall prosper below, but I have purposed to descend today and tomorrow as quietly as possible, and the day after try the natives again with every article that may purchase food, even ivory. We must get food then peacefully or forcibly.

The events of the next days are entered under February 21*st.*

February 21*st:*

On the morning of the 19th, we regarded each other mostly as destined victims of protracted famine, or the rage of savage natives. But as we feared famine most, we determined to try the natives. We saw a few fishermen on an island and mildly showed our several kinds of monies to them. Cloth, beads, wire, copper, ivory, iron, et cetera. They frightened ran to the woods, bawling out some words which we could not understand. Two miles further came to a small island opposite a settlement, and without paying regard to the small canoes plying about, we beached our canoes and began to build a camp. Presently a canoe with 7 men came dashing across and we prepared with monies in view of them, unhesitatingly beached their canoes amongst our own [*sic*]. This was one sure auspicious sign of confidence. We were liberal, the natives fearlessly accepted beads and shells we gave them, and then went a step further; we sealed this growing peace with the ceremony of blood brotherhood and interchange of gifts. Still, the first day food came but slowly, as there were three Chiefs to be satisfied . . . The second day food came abundantly and on the 21st goats, wine were added to our necessities. Cloth was the universal demand. Black, Red, and Blue blanketry, Madrassees, Merikani, Kaniki, handkerchiefs and Kitambis. Brass tacks, brass bands, wire, plates, cups, knives, looking-glasses. All had guns, old American flintlocks, overloaded with brass bands and brass tacks and, worn suspended by broad bands of the red buffalo hide, murderously long knives.

It was most difficult to understand them, but we did very well with signs. It was also a difficult task to induce one native to stay long enough for a social chat. But on the morning of the third day, trade lagging, one was discovered patient enough to sit and give such information as I desired.

My notebook was in great demand and would have found a ready sale, they called it Tara Tara or Looking-glass, which they believed came from above.

The voyage was resumed next day. On February 24th Stanley noted in the corner of his sketch map for the day's journey: Hippopotamus attacked a canoe and snatched a paddle from a man's hand, and almost upset the heaviest canoe we had. I believe he was so ferocious at sight of the donkeys, believing they were young of his tribe.

On the night of February 27th at 7 p.m. Stanley observed an eclipse of the Moon. In his notebook for some time he had been one day out in his dating. The following dates are amended accordingly.

March 1st:

On the 1st March about 2 p.m. we arrived in Lat 2°.48′.35″ by observation, about 2 miles north of the Chief of Chumbiri's village. As we neared the rocky point it looked to us, accustomed lately to an enormous breadth of water, low lands and islands, as if an obstacle lay before us. We therefore approached the rocky point of Bateke on the right bank very cautiously and looked eagerly out for opportunities to speak to and obtain information from the natives. Such an opportunity presented itself for on rounding the rocky point three natives were seen running along the rocky shore as if they desired to speak. We dropped anchor about 100 yards from the shore and opening a conversation, by slow degrees and patience obtained a little of their confidence. What they told us here, they a little varied afterwards, though it was welcome to be told that the Cataract was still 5 days off. They readily subscribed to all the demands that strangers seeking security and peace required, the ceremony of blood brotherhood was gone through, through an embassy I sent ashore, and then we were all requested to land and camp. Meantime, the three natives by their halloing had brought about 50 more, and had sent messengers to the old King of Chumbiri opposite that strangers seeking food had arrived. The king sent 3 of his sons across to us with his spear to offer us welcome which we gratefully received and returned with a gift of cloths.

March 2nd:

About 9 a.m. the King in person came accompanied by about 50 people in 4 canoes and at once we perceived that he was a person on whose proffered friendship we could rely. He wore the usual tall hat of chiefs with the other kingly appointments, such as an elephant's tail to brush off flies, medicine and tobacco gourds. A most ceremonious old fellow with a long chibouque which went the rounds of his Courtiers, who surrounded him with submissive and loyal faces.

During our very friendly interview, he invited me over to the left bank to his own village, and gave such cogent reasons for his invitation that we gladly complied. At 2 p.m. we landed on a sandy beach near his village and were welcomed by his people with demonstrations of great friendship. Frank at my request went through the ceremony of blood brotherhood with him, after which there was no necessity for suspicion. According to him:

> Misongo was 3 days from Chumbiri
> Nkunda   7 days from Misongo
> Cataract   10 days from Nkunda.

March 4th:

Halt at Chumbiri, Uyanza.

The king after saying he would give me guides as far as the Cataract for 5 *doti*, changed his mind and the extent of what he finally received after a tedious chatter was 6 cloths for himself, one coil of wire, 100 cowries. Three cloths for his sons and 960 cowries for the paddlers, besides the return of 2 goats he had given me yesterday.

He is, though old and of a kindly aspect, a prodigious liar, and his people are cunning beyond description. Their merit lies in the kind reception they give to strangers.

March 5th:

Halt.

A native accused of witchcraft was drowned according to doom today: arms tied behind, and a wooden gag in his mouth, thrown into a canoe and paddled into the river and tossed overboard. As he was tossed, the executioner cried out to him: "If you are a Magician, cause this river to dry up and save yourself." After a few seconds he rose again and was carried down the stream about half a mile. A huge crocodile, fat with prey, followed him slowly and then rushed on him and we saw him no more.

March 6th:

Halt.

This day we had proposed to continue our journey, but our guides to the Cataract of Nkunda held off and hid themselves until nearly night. We heard that they were discontented with their hire, and demanded 2000 cowries more. After some hesitation and a pledge, the King's spear, given into our hands that they would keep their promise, I paid them 2000 cowries.

March 7th:

Crossed river to right bank at 4 p.m. Rain came on. Guides (3 canoes), 45 people and we halted, made rough sleeping huts. Midnight, guides made their charms and called upon their spirit to guide us safely from camp to camp, which they named. Having seen them charm away the rain, our Wangwana had a growing faith in them.

March 8th:

Our journey today has been about 12 miles.

We started with the guides from Chumbiri with fair hopes that we should continue together, that they should be faithful to their trust. They had performed ceremonies during the night to appease their God and to induce him to give them his protection on the journey. About 8 a.m. a violent rainstorm lasting 4 hours began. Noon we tried it again, but an hour afterwards they halted again and told us to continue on. Though suspecting strongly that they were intending to leave us, we proceeded until nearly sunset. In the night a boa constrictor 12 feet long was seen advancing towards one of the men. The man hailed it thinking it to be a man as it raised itself, and asked who he was, but instantly perceived his mistake and screamed: "A serpent! A serpent!" At the noise the boa glided away, but in about half an hour was seen in another part of the camp, and this time after a good deal of noise was despatched.

March 9th:

Voyage continues [*past Mwana Ibaka*].

Today the 32nd fight occurred on this river, without any cause further than the savage wilfulness of the natives. In this fight we had 3 wounded in the boat and one in the canoe. Having driven our enemies to the shelter of their woods, we proceeded on our way until we came to an island where we halted for about 4 hours, waiting for our guides who presently appeared. We followed them to a village on the left bank but the natives, though they admitted our guides, took position along the shore to fight us, while the guides made violent motions for us to continue on our way which we did, not wishing to fight without cause or to annoy the natives wilfully. We camped about 3 miles below on the right bank. About dusk our guides camped on the left bank opposite. Our wounded we attended to, and found the wounds but slight.

March 10*th:*

Voyage continues.

The guides this morning departed from their camp on the left bank, at the same time we left our camp on the right bank, but they would hold no conversation with us, until about 10 a.m. when they changed their minds, crossed the river and began to cook their food. We were then permitted to speak with them, when they clamorously excused themselves from being the cause of the violent conduct of the natives of Mwana Ibaka. We readily excused them and then took an opportunity of offering more money to them upon arriving at the Cataract, but they wished it to be given them there and then, but we having already paid them for their services which were as yet but partially given, and the prospect very poor of their doing any more, gave them up and proceeded on our way alone. At night we camped alone about 9 miles below in a cove between two precipitous cliffs.

The journey continued without help of guides.

March 13*th:*

Halt above Cataract.

At about noon the river widened until it resembled a Lake with numerous sandy bars, islets, and several wooded islands. On the right bank there was a wall of cliffs—chalk—resembling Dover Cliffs so greatly that I have named them after them in order to distinguish and guide the future traveller.

Then descending along the right bank near the first Falls opposite Ntamo we encountered very peaceable people in canoes who spoke kindly and came near, unsuspicious and confident, to us, to speak with us which we took to be a good omen. A little above the first breaking of the water we camped . . .

March 14*th:*

The Chief of Ntamo with a large retinue in two canoes came to visit us, gave us presents of food which were very welcome and for a large Manyema goat of which he would not be denied, he made blood brotherhood with Frank and sealed it with his *kisi* or medicine.

March 15*th:*

About 10 a.m. we were visited by the King of Nkunda, the Chief of the Bateke west of Dover Cliffs, the Chief of the Bateke at the Falls and finally by the King of Ntamo. We had four Kings at our levee, all of whom brought presents and gifts— goats, chickens, bananas, cassava and bread, and who received suitable presents in return. The King of Ntamo was very urgent that we should return at some future time and make trade with him, but opposed to our proceeding higher up the river and his village. This arose, of course, from a fear that he would lose his profits. His *kisi*, or medicine, was in great request to prohibit us from venturing higher up should we ever return.

About 4 p.m. we began our descent of the Falls and descended half a mile.

This widening of the River Congo was to be known to future travellers as Stanley Pool. The medicine of the King of Ntamo was not wholly without effect, for thanks to Stanley's activities when organizing the Congo Free State, the opposing shores of the Pool became the sites for the modern commercial cities of Leopoldville and Brazzaville. The Falls below the Pool he named after David Livingstone. From Nyangwe to Ntamo and the Falls, Stanley had traced the River Congo for 1,235 miles.

March 16*th:*

Continued on our work, and descended half a mile or $\frac{3}{4}$ of a mile to the River Juemba which issues into the Congo from the right bank just at the Falls. We have some skilful work to do to dare the mighty current round the rocky points, and lower the canoes by hawsers, which, had one broken, would have certainly been the destruction of the canoe and the men in it, for only a few yards below rushes the river with enormous leaping waves into a brown abyss of mad waters and rocks and foam. Having arrived in the Juemba we paddled desperately across to an island and here our labours ended for the day.

March 17th:

Dragged the canoes across Juemba Island to the western branch of the Juemba River, distance about 800 yards. Chief of Bateke Manoweh visited me and for a small gratuity of cloth repaid with small supply of food became fast friends. People very hungry. If none can be procured tomorrow we must despatch the riding asses.

March 18th:

Descended the west branch of the Juemba River to its junction with the Congo about half a mile and then camped. People fainted for lack of food. We had to stay work to allow them to hunt for food. They were successful and made tolerably good marketing. A goat is not to be seen in the country and a chicken is to be esteemed at the value of a gun, but cassava is abundant.

March 19th:

Crossed the point of land with the canoes which is west of the confluence of the Juemba and Congo, and placed the canoes in a creek. The natives continue friendly though the numerous chiefs are expensive. However they bring us food and so long as matters stand thus, we may be content. Accidents were numerous the first day. One dislocated his shoulder, another cut his foot badly on the rough rocks, legs and feet were cut.

March 20th:

From the Creek crossed a sand bar 300 yards wide into the Congo, thence punted the canoes along shore down about 800 yards to an inlet above a point of rocks.

March 21st:

Prepared a road overland across point of rocks to river inlet and drew canoes up from inlet 100 feet up on land. The road is fully ¾ mile long over enormous rocks most part, toughest job yet before us tomorrow. Natives bring food and peaceful trade continues.

March 22nd:

Crossed the Rocky Point, placed our canoes in the Congo and paddled down half a mile to the extreme corner of Western Reach of River.

March 24th:

Halt for rest to the wearied people.

March 25th:

We set to work at daybreak with the canoes to lower them down the Rapids, but alas we were only able to do half a mile. We lost our best canoe, 75 feet long 3 feet wide by 21 inches deep, the Rapids were too strong for us. At evening a canoe parted from us was upset, sent back half a mile, sent to the current, again ejected half a mile and finally to our great joy secured. Another canoe was almost totally ruined but we have patched it up and it may serve. Horrible and slow work. All my energies are engaged in it.

March 26th:

Got 5 canoes and boat down Cauldron to Camp near Rocky Island. Our best remaining canoe broke its cane cables as we lowered it, was swept down the Cauldron, heaved up, whirled round in quick gyrations and finally sent into bay near our camp where it was finally secured. One Chief had his great toe crushed, a man was pitched on his head by the waves, and while turning round after the fearful day's labour I suddenly dropped down to my astonishment into a pit among the great rocks 25 feet deep, escaping thankfully with my life, with only a few rib bruises to remind me that it was bad policy to be careless in such dangerous places.

The Cauldron was a particularly dangerous stretch of water between the Upper and Lower Falls.

March 27th:

Got rest of canoes to camp.

March 28th:

Lowered canoes down to bend opposite Rocky Island and Falls.

The great River of Congo which we but late admired for its lake-like breadth on which we glided so smoothly is now a maddened flood, its free flow restrained by huge walls of basaltic boulders and caked lava. It roars its anger incessantly, and bounds down its steep interrupted bed like a contracted angry sea between cliffs.

March 29th:

From this bend at daybreak we began to punt the canoes close to the rocks until we reached the Falls, then cut bushes and overlaid a point of rocks with them and made a kind of tramway, for in this work we were now experienced. By noon we had crossed the point with our 13 canoes and boat all of which were got safely and without accident in a little cove protected by the Rocky Point. Our next labour was apparently easy. I had sent a man the day previous to examine the river as far as the bend where we intended to camp, and he reported that by clinging to the right bank there was not the slightest danger. I instructed the people to keep close to the right bank and by no means to venture into the strong heaving current. This, "Please God", they proposed to do.

The boat as usual led the way and got safely into the bend, followed by 3 canoes. The fourth canoe over 80 feet long was manned by six paddlers [*including the boy Kalulu*] . . . Rehani the steersman did not observe my instructions, the current wafted him slowly into the middle of the mighty river where human strength availed nothing and the canoe and its unfortunate people glided by over the treacherous calm surface like an arrow to doom. It soon reached the island which cleft the Falls, and swept to the left branch, was whirled round three or four times, and presently we saw the stern of the canoe pointed upward and knew then that only by a miracle could any of the crew be saved.

Fast upon this catastrophe, before we could begin to wail their loss, another canoe with two men darted by, borne by like lightning on the bosom of the placid but irresistible waters to apparent nay almost certain destruction. We shouted out to them commands to make for the left shore. "Inshallah", the steersmen replied, and vigorously the two men set to work. By a strange chance or his dexterity, he shot his canoe over the Falls, and lower down in calmer water he contrived to secure his canoe to the shore. [*These were Wadi Ambari and Mabruki.*]

The two men were presently seen clambering over the rocks towards the point opposite our camp, and finally to sit down regarding us in silence, so far as we knew. Our pity and love gushed strong towards them, but we could utter nothing of it. The roar of the Falls mocked and overpowered the feeble human voice.

In the hope to save the rest of the canoes, for there were still two behind, 8 having arrived safely, I despatched a messenger to instruct the crews not to trust to their paddles alone but to have in each small canoe two men to tow the canoe by cane ropes on shore and two in each canoe with paddles and poles to keep from striking against rocks. The messenger returned with their reply that they would observe all precaution, but he had no sooner done speaking than a third canoe darted past with only one man, a young fellow called Soudi of Ituru who knew nothing of steering, but who paddled his canoe as if by instinct. As he passed us, he shouted to me: "I am lost, Master; there is but one God". He then was seen to address himself to what Fate had in store for him.

The river swept him down, down over the First Falls, then gave him a breathing pause in dead water, again caught him and his canoe in its tremendous force, precipitated him down, over the second and the third and fourth falls, great waves meanwhile striking madly at him, and yet his canoe did not sink, but he and it were seen to sweep behind the island and we could see nothing more, for darkness fell on us and on the river.

It is said that the cause of this last accident was the faithlessness of the crew. One man, unnerved by what he saw, ran away and hid in the bushes, another let go the tow rope, and the other rope, too weak to resist the sudden forces and weight, snapped, and thus the man is probably lost.

During the night a large canoe was swept from its mooring by a sudden tide, and this has closed our losses for this day.

We have now but 9 canoes and the boat left, inadequate to carry the Expedition. Some of the people must, therefore, go on land.

March 30th:

Halt for rest.

No news of the lost, except that the two men on the opposite side have been in view lying on the rocks. They have nothing to eat, they therefore must suffer, though were they alive to their interests they might barter with the friendly natives a part of their dress.

Today as previously I have been exploring ahead a long distance, and so far I see no immediate likelihood of this work coming to an end.

March 31st:

Descended 1½ miles to South-south-west end of Kalulu Island and Falls. No news of the lost men. Natives amiable. Food abundant and cheap. No symptoms yet of the river's abating its resistless wave and roar. We are almost stunned with the river's uproar and turbulent waters.

April 1st:

Descended and cleared Kalulu Falls and camped on right bank a little below.

Our two absentees are on the opposite side signalling frequently to us but we cannot assist them.

April 2nd:

Descended a mile and a half of rapids, two more canoes received great injuries, one of which probably may be lost.

About 2 p.m. the two absentees [*Wadi Ambari and Mabruki*] made their appearance in our camp to our general joy, bringing with them young Soudi of Ituru who had gone through strange adventures. He had been swept down by the fierce current and whirled round so often that he was almost giddy, then finally landed far below, just at night, on the summit of a lone rock.

Tying his canoe so that it might not be swept away, he swam ashore, and was immediately seized by a man on landing and dragged inland several hours' journey in the night. He was taken to a hut and stripped naked for a personal examination. The captor congratulated himself upon the personal appearance

The village of Manyema from a sketch by the author.
From the Illustrated London News

Battle on the Lualaba.
From the Illustrated London News

Zanzibar, a photograph by the author.
Richard Stanley

Journey's end—the arrival at Kabinda.
Photograph: J. Silveira, St Paul de Loanda, 1877

of his slave, for Soudi was handsome and a great favourite with the female wantons of Ujiji. He was then fed with manioc and fish and told to go to sleep, but in the night, Soudi was heard digging his way to freedom and the man bound him.

Next morning the captor informed his neighbours of the merits of his prize and many came to view him, among whom was a subject of King Itsi of Ntamo who at once drew such a terrible picture of a White Man with large fiery eyes and long black hair who possessed a whole armour of quick-firing and strange guns and a little instrument around his waist which [*killed?*] any number of men at once, that it was a danger to the entire country to detain any of his men. This so frightened him that he at once led Soudi of Ituru with a cord round his waist to the Falls near which he found him. "Go", said he, "to your King, here is food for you until he comes, but do not tell him, I entreat of you, that I placed you in bonds. Tell him I fed you and he will be pleased with us." Thus brave young Soudi got his liberty and was restored to me and his comrades.

Wadi Ambari and Mabruki were obliged to hide an entire day in the woods to prevent being enslaved.

When the three were met, they were greatly encouraged and on Soudi informing his two friends that his canoe was safe, the three made up their minds to cross the river rather than endure any further anxiety. Despair gave them courage, and though they were [*carried?*] with the speed of an arrow for several miles, they finally landed on the left bank and having hid their canoe trudged up to meet us.

April 3rd:

Descended a mile and a half of rapids and camped at the South-west corner of Relief Bay.

One canoe was upset and a bag of beads lost, otherwise no other accident. Natives fortunately still continue friendly and sell food cheap. No news of the lost 6, and I fear I must give them up for lost, poor fellows. My heart aches sorely for them especially for Rehani . . . and Kalulu. But it is such a dangerous career we now run, accidents are so numerous and daily, and I myself run daily three or four startling adventures, that we have scarcely space or time to wail or weep. Peace to them, and I pray we may have it (for it is a sad life) when we die.

April 4th & 5th:

Halt 2 days for repairs to canoes and boat.

No news of absent men or canoes. Natives continue amiable enough. Lemons sold to us at this camp by natives and a species of fruit similar to the *Nux Vomica*, but containing a red pulpy matter.

April 6th:

Descended one mile, a canoe sunk but recovered.
Goats numerous, but not to be sold; chickens dear.
Soudi Ituru's canoe lost.

April 7th:

Descended 2 miles. No accident today.

April 8th:

Descended half a mile with canoes, as far as Whirlpool Narrows. There finding that the eddy tides rushing up river round the point required delicate skilful manoeuvring, we contented ourselves with experimenting on the boat first. Twice she snapped ropes and cables and flew up river borne on the crests of brown waves with but two men and a boy.

"Take to your oars when she stops, and return to the Bay," I shouted out to them as they passed by me. "Please God," Uledi cheerily replied. By and by the boat stopped, of course, where the flow and the ebb met and at once oars swept the boat back to us.

We tried the boat again with six cables of twisted cane, about 200 feet in length each, five men to each cable. The rocks rose singly in precipitous masses 30 feet above the river and this added to the difficulty. Footing was precarious and the furious eddies and whirlpools during the rainy season had drilled pits—circular—and ovens 4, 6 and 10 feet deep. However, with the utmost patience we succeeded in rounding these enormous blocks and in braving the brown waves of the furious eddy tide, and bringing the boat to where the water resumed its natural downward flow. Below this were some two miles of boisterous water close to the rocky shore, close to which it was dangerous to bring the boat. It remained then to shoot the rapids in mid-river, and the boat's crew gallantly volunteered, headed by Uledi, to take her to camp 2 miles below. Two men took hold of the stern cable, while the crew took their seats. When they were all prepared, oars in hand, the cable was cut and the boat was borne by the impetuous current to mid-stream, and in a few minutes they were abreast of the camp, where by laying on their oars, they succeeded in bringing the boat to camp, instilling courage in the minds of the canoe crews who were to do the same feat on the morrow.

April 9th:

Shot the rapids today with our 9 canoes successfully. Frank took 3 canoes over the same ground in first rate style. Our canoe with 6 men was swept within 200 yards of the Falls of Round Island, and one man was half drowned but was saved by Frank and Zambarao, who paddled out to the river to save him after he had sunk once.

April 10th:

Lowered the boat 2 miles and conveyed goods to camp. After section of boat sank at Falls—lower part of Round Island Falls—and got jammed between 2 rocks, we were about 2 hours freeing her from her perilous position, but finally succeeded with little injury to her. Two men had a narrow escape from being swept [*away*] by the falls, but they caught hold of a cable—cane—as they were apparently hurrying to their doom. The canoes have been reserved for tomorrow.

April 11th:

Lowered canoes without accident to camp, and then embarked goods and camped west end of Gavubu's Bay.

April 12th:

Conveyed goods on shore from Gavubu's Bay to Gamfwa's Bay and brought boat and canoes there also by noon without accident—1 mile journey. After breakfasting, embarked goods and landed them at west end of Gamfwa's Bay and after discharging boat started the descent to the last camp for the day, which was about 1½ miles below. Cane cables were lashed bow and stern and three men had hold of each, we then began the descent as cautiously and skilfully as a month's experience of a most dangerous series of Falls and Rapids had taught us. But we had a worse place than usual to contend with. Before us were long lines of brown white-topped breakers without any little indentation in the rocky shore to give us breath; so that the boat was urged along too rapidly and dragged the men behind too swiftly, before they could secure their footing. Finally, to check the threatening hurried descent, the men were compelled to lie down on the rocks, but this was not enough. The boat dragged them over the boulders into the water. Her stern sheered further into the stream and then it was all up.

One man was jerked amongst the swift descending breakers. The others let go, fearing the same fate, the bow cable parted and the boat with me, two boys and two men, was flying down the mighty and terrible stream borne on the crests of great waves, whirled round like a spinning top, diving into threatening troughs, and swirling pits, then jostled aside, uplifted by another wave and tossed upon the summit of another, while the shore was flying by us with amazing rapidity, which we could not reach. The boat also leaked so badly to which we could give no attention that it was another element of danger.

We soon came in view of a bend in the land where I had purposed to camp, and below the river looked wilder than ever. Could we but get within the influence of the eddy tide, we might be saved. We devoted all our energies to enter within its influence, across the swift gliding waters.

As we began to feel that it was useless to contend with the current, a sudden terrible rumbling noise caused us to look below, and we saw the river almost heaved bodily upward, as if a volcano had burst under it. It took the form of a low shapeless mound, and presently half of the mass approached us in lines of white breakers, gurgling bodies separated by so many whirling pools, one of which caught and embraced our poor shattered way-worn boat, by which we were spun around and around and around with the stern threatening each moment to drop into the centre of the wide pit, until finally we were spun out of it into the ebb tide and so were saved. The people were almost in despair and were rushing after us distractedly, but long before they reached us they met a man whom I sent to inform them of our safety.

The man who was dragged into the water, I saved.

April 13*th:*

This day was occupied in lowering the canoes down the rapids by Gamfwa's. It was most delicate and dangerous work. Every hour almost was remarkable for its special accident, a man bruised, or a man almost drowned, or a canoe swept into the river and saved by a miracle, or a canoe irrecoverably lost. One small canoe was lost, one with a man within was flooded with water, swept down 2 miles, sunk in a whirlpool, canoe came to the surface a hundred yards from the man, but finally the man being an expert swimmer recovered his seat on the keel of the canoe and both after an age of anxiety were saved. One canoe was smashed, but possibly may be saved. The great canoe has been left for tomorrow's work.

April 14*th:*

Descended one mile to the Nkenke River Bay, safely.

We heard the roar of water tonight on each side of us. The Congo has two slight falls, one in front and one behind. The Nkenke's Falls are worth seeing and they are just 100 yards from us, and a Cataract falls into the Congo on the opposite side.

The Expedition halted for 2 days for repairs.

April 17*th:*

Descended three miles by shooting the rapids.

One canoe was irrecoverably smashed, and a large canoe which broke away from us during the night at Kalulu Falls was recovered from the Bateke, who had picked her up as she was slowly gliding along the eddy tide . . .

We have discovered we are one bag of Blue Mutoonda [*beads*] short. It most certainly must have been stolen by our own people. I propose to make a general search tomorrow.

April 18*th:*

Descend 1 mile by shooting rapids to a snug little cove beyond place where canoe was restored.

The earlier part of the morning was spent in examining the goods and luggage of the people. About three *kbete* of Amber Mutoonda beads were found. Where the other sack of Blue is gone I have not discovered. [*Five men*] were flogged for stealing.

The sound of the rapids about here is like the swash of water about a ship's bows as she flies before a spanking breeze.

April 19th:

Shot ½ a mile of dangerous rapids and whirlpools, then loaded canoes with goods and pulled down about 2½ miles of very fair water.

It's bad by river and bad by land, the banks are towering hills, steep, abrupt, sometimes cliffy, between which and the river, on either side, are enormous masses of blackened, worn, sometimes riven rock, some 20 feet high, over which we must labour with the loads overland, for we dare not trust to the rapids with our means of sustenance and defence, nor dare we scale the abrupt or steep hills of 1,200 or 1,500 feet.

We have arrived at Yellala, but the prospect as I can make it with my field glass looks bad, and is confirmed by exploration ahead. Natives say a great Cataract is ahead.

April 20th:

Pulled down with oars past 2 or 3 small isolated falls. 2½ miles opposite Nsangu.

On right bank a small river falls over a sheet of rock 300 or 400 feet high into the Congo.

Wild pineapples and lemons abundant. Pigs abundant but dear. Three or four cloths or a gun asked for one. A goat is also 3 *doti*—or a gun.

Cloth is so abundant in this region that it is against our conscience to give our cloth away, fearful when we are so scarce of some inconvenience ahead. We consequently limit ourselves to a chicken a day when procurable, which is not always.

April 21st:

Halt for rest and to explore right bank ahead.

Natives report a fearful Cataract and impassable bank of

cliff walls. To prevent rushing into such a dangerous locality, I sent 5 men with instructions to travel far and examine the banks.

April 22nd:

Pulled down river with oars 1¾ miles to camp over Hill Island south-west of Nsangu. Carried as usual goods overland, but arrived at camp early.

April 23rd:

Shot Hilly Island Rapids and then pulled to camp one mile opposite lower end of Hilly Island. Sent Kacheche and five men to reach Great Cataract ahead and to report upon prospect of getting past it.

Today ends the 35th mile of rapids, falls and cataracts according to calculation by estimate.

It had taken them 37 days.

April 24th:

Descend from lower end of Hilly Island 1¾ miles to camp. Shot two dangerous rapids with canoes and boat, no accident, I am thankful.

April 25th:

Descend half a mile, then camp. I explore ahead, and perceive no road by river or near its banks. I therefore determine upon a mountain route 1,200 feet high, and point out the path.

April 26th:

Hauled 6 canoes up the mountain between sunrise and sunset to the utter amazement of the natives on the tableland who believed that I intended to march the Expedition with a canoe train for the future overland. Our hostile, and fearful friends opposite took position early in the morning to see us shoot the Falls and perish in the brown billows of the Congo, but they have not been able to make up their minds yet why we allowed such a bright day for such a spectacle to pass idly away. The six men whom I sent 4 days ago to explore the terrible Cataract reported lately to us, returned today at sunset and were told by fearful natives that the White Chief was carrying his canoes over the mountains, and they were seen locking and tying their hogs up and removing valuable things away further inland, and fastening their doors, and preparing with resignation and fortitude for the dreadful results of such a wild undertaking.

The report of my explorers is rather encouraging, but it will not do to build too high hopes upon them, for the principal of them is liable to exaggerate favourably as others of his class are to exaggerate opposite.

April 27th:

On the tableland. Moved canoes about 500 yards higher up.

April 28th:

Moved canoes about 500 yards higher up, to the highest part of the tableland 1,400 feet above river. Progress made about 700 yards.

Natives friendly. Food plentiful but meat scarce.

April 29th:

Halt for rest.

Onions seen today in camp. Moth-flies ate white ants greedily on an anthill. Wangwana saw them and fastened on them.

April 30th:

Hauled canoes up hill. Aneroid shows 1,900 feet undeducted.

May 1st:

Marched 3 miles over mountains and descended with goods to the river, leaving Manwa Sera with 80 men to drag the canoes after us, while I and my artisans should construct a new canoe.

May 2nd:

In camp by river.

Cut a Ubani tree [*Burseracea Boswellia, the gum-frankincense*] down to construct a canoe, but the tree has fallen across a gigantic rock, and we are now at our wits end to get this big tree—10 feet 5 inches round—to the ground from the rock.

May 3rd:

In camp by river.

Making canoe after successfully landing it below from rock, but I fear some trouble and annoyances from the natives.

May 4th:

Nzabi. In camp by river.

Making canoe. Chief of Nzabi paid his visit, brought gifts of palm wine and bananas, which were reciprocated. No trouble, as was expected, but the Chief offered to show us another tree.

Stanley and the advance party stayed in Nzabi working on their canoe and waiting for the main body of the Expedition to arrive by the overland route.

May 10th:

Canoes and people arrive at Nzabi after their long overland march.

May 11th:

Nzabi.

Dragged our new canoe into water and tested it. Tolerably good and swift, but requires a little more work. One of our men Saburi Rehani has been apprehended by natives on charge of stealing a chicken. Negotiations have been begun for his release but not terminated.

May 12th:

Lowered canoes down 1 mile to Nzabi Creek. I am told there are 5 Falls yet. Saburi Rehani deserted from his captors and came to camp, but lest violence and revenge may ensue, I have decided to send him back tomorrow with a fine to pay them. Our new canoe was launched today and on her first trial trip did well, but the second time she capsized and one man narrowly escaped drowning.

May 13th:

Nzabi Creek.

Far from being offended at our cutting the finest tree of the forest for our canoe, the King and natives have been at great pains to find us another still larger—circumference 13 feet 3 inches—which as we are in need of one more canoe to replace some of the small ones lost, we cut down today. This will probably delay us about 10 days longer, but as we have a fall opposite us, Nseto Falls—two days at least would be lost anyhow.

In order to hurry up the work I have set a night party under Frank and a Chief.

Work continued on the second canoe for the next 4 days.

May 18th:

Nzabi Creek.

Sixth day at work on 2nd canoe. Attempted to turn her over this morning, was not able. Began work again to reduce her. Succeeded in the afternoon after immense effort with 100 men.

We almost got into a row by accident. Kacheche was sent to the blacksmith's to repair axes. The blacksmith's children were playing about close to their father while at work, and a red hot iron flew from his hand against a little girl's breast. The war drum was beaten, but the Chief of Nzabi stood fast our friend and compromised the difficulty with a fine of 15 cowries.

Ship building continued. On May 20th the Expedition received the first news of Europeans down-river. On May 22nd the second canoe was launched and was found to be remarkably speedy. It carried 60 people and measured 54 feet in length. On May 24th the Expedition left Nzabi Creek and on May 25th while the debilitated members travelled by water, Stanley and the more robust marched 3 miles over the plateau to Mowa:.

Boat had a narrow escape at the Upper Mowa Falls, plunged headfirst and smashed a hole in her stern. Frank Pocock, lame from ulcers in the feet was in her. Three canoes were got safely to camp between Upper and Lower Falls.

Natives amiable and pretend to great knowledge of the down river ports.

Having safely negotiated the Upper and Lower Falls, the Expedition halted in Mowa Cove to repair the canoes and explore the river ahead. Stanley complained of the thievishness of his own men, as also that of the natives who besides stealing a hammer have even stolen a screw bolt from the boat.

June 1st:

Mowa Cove.
Found a treasure of bees-wax today through the natives.

June 2nd:

Mowa Cove.
The bees located on high boulders along the river bank. The bees are short stunted harmless things. The natives say that the honey is made by the eye flies.

The natives of East Mowa are considerably excited today because I took my notebook out and wrote the names of things in their dialect. They say I made strong medicine to kill their country and give it to a young [*Mowa*] friend of ours who has been industrious to please and consequently has been favoured by me.

June 3rd:

A BLACK WOEFUL DAY! We had all enjoyed a pleasant rest from hard labours and today we were prepared to toil our way through the few remaining Falls without pause until we should reach the calm river a few miles below, and last night Frank Pocock had been called to my tent where we chatted pleasantly and sociably about the near end of our struggles through the Congo Falls, also of the hopeful termination of our many dangerous toils. Frank had been for many days a victim to ulcerous feet, which made him unable to lend us aid, but he was none the less useful to me because, though he could not oversee the men at their labours, he could stay in camp to watch the goods, and to see that no skulkers were absent from duty.

This morning the men shouldered the goods and baggage and under Kacheche marched overland 3 miles to Zinga, while I resolved to attempt the passage down two small Falls, the Massesse and Massassa, in the *Lady Alice* with the boat's crew. Clinging close to the shore, we rowed down ¾ of a mile or thereabouts when we were halted by a lofty precipice, by the sides of which we could travel no further, as the tide, belched to right and left from the centre by the furious waters of the stream escaping down the Mowa Falls, came turning to meet us up river with many a brown wave and heave, and dangerous whirlpools. We then steered for the centre, and fought steadily on against the strong back tide, but it was of no use, and then we thought we would attempt the central stream that rushed with a white foamy face down river. Neither could we reach this, for the boat was heavy and sinking steadily under its growing weight of water, for she was very leaky and the repairs we had made were utterly insufficient.

By observing the shores and the more menacing appearance of the river, I perceived that instead of making any advance down river, we were imperceptibly being drawn towards the terrible whirling pools which almost momently play in the vicinity of the down stream and back tide, where the great waves heaved up by the raging and convulsive centre, and parting to right and left, are opposed by the back-tide flowing strong towards the fearful current.

Presently I saw at a little distance the first symptoms of the swirling vortex. Two floods flowing from different sides, with white brown crests, rush towards each other, the stronger raises its head, strikes and soon engulfs the weaker, which however dies not at once, but heaves upward convulsively, as if a volcano had suddenly burst beneath, into a watery hill which presently subsiding begins circling round with a small hole in the middle large enough for a garden dibble. This rapidly increases in volume, attracts or meets greater accession of force, until a terrible pool in appearance and form like a huge washbasin with the bottom knocked out—fatal to everything floatable that is near its verge or influence—whirling round like a flying wheel is found.

These were the symptoms which I saw, and as I saw the fatal watery pit though whirling still advancing, though advancing still whirling, the deathly snare whence if embraced was no escape, I shouted to oarsmen and steersman to do their best, or prepare to die. Meantime I threw off my coat and belts, and prepared for the worst. The oars bent under the sturdy efforts as though they would break, but in a few seconds we looked at the pit just over our stern, and a kindly wave near the verge of it drifted us further off. The boat by this time was half full of water, and I gave it up as an impossible task and returned to camp to try my luck in a canoe.

When I came to camp, the men left there were not sufficient to man a canoe, and I was compelled to proceed overland after the goods, not before telling my Captain, Manwa Sera, to send a rescue canoe with long cords to Zinga, where just below the Massassa Falls it might lie ready to lend a helping hand in case of accident. I talked with Frank before setting out about the difficulty, but that with great care and clinging close to the land with hauling ropes, the journey might easily be done by water.

In the afternoon I sat on the rocks of Zinga looking up river with field-glass in hand, and after long waiting I saw a canoe upset with 8 heads above water. Kacheche and Wadi Rehani were at once sent along the rocks to render any possible aid. Meanwhile I watched the men in the water, as they were borne into the basin of Bolo-Bolo by the spreading current. I saw their struggles to right her, I saw them raise themselves on the keel of the canoe and paddling. Finally I saw them land, but the canoe was swept down river over the Zinga Falls, then over the Ingulufi Falls, then away out of sight.

Bad news travels fast. I soon heard the names of the saved and those of the drowned. Among the latter was Frank Pocock, my servant, my companion and good friend.

Alas, my brave, honest, kindly-natured, good Frank, thy many faithful services to me have only found thee a grave in the wild waters of the Congo. Thy many years of travel and toil and danger borne so cheerfully have been but ill-rewarded. Thou Noble Son of Nature, would that I could have suffered instead of thee for I am weary, Oh so weary of this constant tale of woes and death; and thy cheerful society, the influence of thy brave smile, the utterance of thy courageous heart I shall lack, and because I lack, I shall weep for my dear lost friend.

"And weep the more because I weep in vain."

It appears from the statements of the men and Uledi the Coxswain of the *Lady Alice*, that Frank, perceiving the rescue canoe about setting out, said that he could not wait for a second canoe but would go with the first, and accordingly took his seat and gave the word to set out. The strong back tide against which we had laboured in the morning proved no obstacle to them, for their vessel was swift and well manned. Two miles brought them to the cove between Massesse Falls and Massassa Falls, where the Coxswain told Frank it would be better to land on the rocks and examine the Falls first. Frank assented and sent him and three others to report on it. He was unable to proceed himself as he was troubled with ulcers in the feet.

The men after a long examination said it was a very bad place, that it would be a difficult job to go through.—"Well, what shall I do, I am hungry, and I can't go by land. Must I die here from hunger? You people are so afraid of water that the slightest ripple makes you tremble. Where is the danger of going down the middle stream?" Frank consulting with his men thought there would be no danger by attempting the middle passage and by that road they set off without one presentiment or fear because they were all expert swimmers and divers, and Frank specially excelled in swimming and had often exhibited clever feats in that art, and to their minds Massassa Falls presented no difficulty compared with the many they had hardily passed.

They soon reached the glassy slope of the middle passage and had cleared the fierce yellow waves that seemed to chase them, but here the coxswain thought he would leave midstream and strike for the rocky precipice that lifts its brown front of solid rock a thousand feet into the air above the Bolo-Bolo Basin, and it was at the confluence of the down and back tide that Frank and two of my men met their Fate. The two water forces were just then meeting, they raised their foamy heads and dashed against each madly, and both after this first conflict embraced and subsided and in place of the liquid mound a pit was formed round the rim of which they were wheeled three or four times, during which time Frank tore his shirt off and all prepared for the deadly struggle. The bow of the canoe approached the middle of the pit, was sucked in and every soul was drawn down, down, down until—the survivors said—they thought their breasts would burst from the pent up air within, but after a few seconds the whirlpool relaxed its hold on their feet and they were soon ejected upward to see each other far apart, some saved, and some missing. Uledi and Wadi Baraka say they saw Frank twice above water senseless, the first of whom made a desperate effort to reach him with the tow rope, but it was too short. The two Wangwana they never saw. The most probable reason I can give of Frank's inability to save himself despite the weight of his clothes is that he must while struggling upward have struck his head against the canoe and become stunned; I am somewhat confirmed in this opinion from the fact that Wadi Baraka almost sank under the same canoe, but soon recovering regained his hold and was saved.

At this place we first heard the distinctive titles of the Portuguese, English and French given, and wonder of wonders saw a jacket worn by one of the people.

Often we talked of the probability of the loss of one of us, either by war, sickness, or flood. It was myself who was most likely to be the first victim, as Frank's duty was but to stay in camp to command the garrison. My duty and inclination and anxiety that all should go well led me when important work demanded my presence, a difficult fall, a skilful manoeuvre, [*to go first?*]. The awe the men entertained of me held them to their duty, which either inspired them to activity or wholesomely restrained them. While Frank was regarded more as a friend, I was looked at as a severe, exacting master in whose presence there could be no shirking. It was myself piloted ahead the difficult and dangerous passages and where there was danger no canoe was to follow unless report from me was obtained.

Three times I have narrowly escaped; and had Frank Pocock been well, it was his duty to have followed the goods overland and, thus released from fears of the safety of the goods, my inclination would have led me to superintend the passage of the canoes, and I but waited the appearance of the rescue canoe and the probable safe arrival of Frank to have returned to the scene of operations. I had put all my papers in order, and had informed Frank of what was to be done in the event of my death, for everything so far as I could foresee foretold me that only by special act of Providence could I escape. It was not to be. Though sometimes wishing in my heart that death should overtake me sudden and sharp from the trouble which environed me, by God's grace I was saved.

I do not blame Frank for venturing in the canoe, for in his

position I would have done the same, but it is doubtful that I should have [*tried?*] an unknown dangerous passage before examining it personally, however sick. Frank, besides being brave by nature, had a contempt for the water, bordering on rashness. For instance up river in one day he steered 3 canoes down a most dangerous portion of the river, even against a positive and expressed desire that he should do no more than his own particular duty, that of seeing the canoes manned. His duty was not to steer the canoes, but to see that no skulkers remained on shore.

I do not regard Frank's loss as one that might be looked for. It has been and is a surprise to me that out of 11 men the best swimmer should be lost. I look at it as an extremely unfortunate and regrettable accident, and can only account for it by supposing that in rising from the depth he was made senseless by striking his head against the canoe while submerged. This has been the second day he has taken my place in the river but had I suffered from less anxiety of the safety of the goods, he should not have preceded me.

As I look on his empty tent and dejected servants, and recall to mind his many inestimable qualities, his extraordinary gentleness, his patient temper, his industry, his cheerfulness and tender love of me, the pleasantness of his society, and his general usefulness, I feel myself utterly unable to express my feelings or describe the vastness of my loss. And in looking at the faces of my people, I am certain that their untutored hearts are big with sorrow and sympathise with mine. Every instance of his faithful services to me that I can recall, only intensifies my grief. The long, long companionship in peril thus abruptly severed, his piety, and cheerful trust in a generous Providence suffuses my heart with pity that he departed this life so abruptly and unrewarded for his [*illegible*] . . .

The whole of this entry betrays Stanley's deep distress; parts of it are almost impossible to read; the syntax is incoherent and many of the words are mutilated, as also in the following entry.

June 4th:

Halt at Zinga Falls.

While I sorrow for the loss of my friend Frank I am environed with difficulties. The Chiefs of Mowa are all enraged because they happened to see me writing a few notes, and they have refused to sell food the last two days. Finally one whose rage and grief at the possible disastrous result—of the grave fact of writing notes—to his country, informed us: "If you do not return with that white medicine paper which your King wrote, and tear and burn it before our eyes, you will all die. Go and get it and bring it to us quick." My people, awed and sullen from the recent loss of Frank and two of their companions, sent a man to me to demand it. I gave a sheet of paper scribbled over carelessly to satisfy them, which was torn and burnt, and a smile of relief rewarded us for our complaisance. People sold food to us and visited our camp at Mowa as before. Besides this, I have but 11 men in this camp. Over 90 men are at Mowa sullen and sad. Two Falls lie between that camp and this. The journey over land is long and the days are passing quickly away and soon become months.

June 5th:

Zinga Falls.

Our troubles increase. A messenger from my Captain came today with the stern news that my people had mutinied and refused to work, declaring they would prefer living and hoeing for the heathen than follow the White man longer, for his wages were but the wages of death. The Mowa people, besides covetous of more money despite all I had given, had worked on their fears by talking about the spirits of the Falls who, unless their adorers were appeased, would never cease their wrath but devour all stubborn strangers.

"We," said the heathen, "sacrifice a goat each year to the Spirit of the Falls. You give nothing; how can you hope to escape? Ah, no, give us two tusks of ivory, and we will take your canoes safe beyond all the Falls". On hearing this, the men who are heathen at heart though at Zanzibar they declare they are Moslems, flatly refused to work, though some were forced to obey by Captain Manwa Sera.

A depressing delay ensued.

June 8th:

Zinga Falls.

Held a consultation today with Chiefs about taking the

canoes into the Bolo-Bolo Basin from above Massassa Falls. They, after much drinking of palm wine and inebriate exhibition of fond friendship for self, have decided to try their hand at the work tomorrow. How they will succeed or what will happen God knows. I am almost careless, for my people are so cowardly in the water that I can do nothing with them.

June 9th:

Zinga Falls. Halt.

We are fighting each day but make but little progress in this terrible complicated system of whirlpools, ebb tides and furious down rush of stream such as is found near Mowa, or between Mowa and Massassa, and the precipitous cliffy front of the banks, a thousand feet high, sometimes perpendicular like a wall prohibit all thought of escape by land.

June 10th:

Zinga Falls. Halt.

Today is the 17th day we have expended since we first saw the Mowa Falls, and our canoes are only at Massassa yet and not descended.

The Wangwana try me exceedingly. Since I have lost Frank, I am unable to leave camp to superintend the men at their work. Consequently, they play behind me. If I leave camp, the Chiefs will steal the monies left under one pretence or another. If I send messengers to hurry Manwa Sera up, the messengers idle their time on the road. We have had an instance of this today. Kacheche, the ever faithful express, the detective, knowing how anxious I was about the safety of the men and canoes, was sent before daylight to carry a message and to take three idlers to their work. Two hours afterwards a messenger left camp and overtook them, though the distance is only 3 miles. What could I say? How can I enforce them to their duty, when they are so far from me? I have publicly expressed a desire to die by a quick sharp death, which I think just now would be a mercy compared to what I endure daily. I am vexed each day by thieves, liars, and unconquerable laziness of the Wangwana. I am surrounded by savages who from some superstitious idea may rise to fight at a moment's notice. Weeks are passing swiftly away and the goods are diminishing, until we have but little left, and at the rate we are going, 6 weeks will suffice to bring us at death's door from starvation.

Should any loss happen to me, I earnestly implore my Executors—the proprietors of the *Daily Telegraph* and *New York Herald* or their Agents, when they call up the people to receive their pay, to reflect well what they are doing. The full story of my sufferings and vexations are not told in this journal, but is locked in my breast. The Wangwana deserve to have their wages carefully reckoned and not a cent more than their legitimate due ought to be paid them. They are faithless, lying, thievish, indolent knaves, who only teach a man to despise himself for his folly in attempting a grand work with such miserable slaves. Slavery is abhorrent to my very soul, and all men engaged in the trade should be doomed to instant death, but these men make me regard myself every day as only a grade higher than a miserable slave driver. Ah Frank! You are happy, my friend. Out of this dreadful mess. Out of this pit of misery in which I am plunged neck deep.

June 11*th:*

Halt. Zinga Falls.
The body of my faithful servant Frank was seen by the natives of Mbelo three days ago early in the morning as it was floating down river. He was lying on his back. Upper part of body nude—he having torn his shirt away to swim—dressings on his feet and pantaloons as he wore them. The natives to my great regret did not secure the body, but left it floating, a dishonoured spectacle on the surface of the river. They said they feared it. My friends of Zinga regretted that the body of a guest of theirs was not recovered for respectful burial.

Stanley was due for a bout of fever, but this notwithstanding he continued his efforts to bring the canoes from up river.

June 15*th:*

Halt. Zinga Falls.
Crossed over hills to Massassa Falls. Work is fearfully slow, useless to preach, talk, beg, threaten, or punish. The people seem to be vowed to indolence and apathy. Goods diminished so fast that I am fear-stricken and weighed down with anxiety.

195

To save myself and a brave few I must sacrifice about 110 lives and even at the last moment I do not think I could be capable of it. Better, far better to die as we have lived together and share fate, even the most fearful. Yet my people anger me, oh so much, and yet I pity and love them. The greatest feeling they provoke in me is astonishment of their apathy. One man, never remarkable for bravery, fidelity, or anything else save his size, told me flatly today: "That they were tired". If tired, why do they not band together and resolutely cut the bonds of attachment, and leave me to pursue my journey alone?

Stanley continued his efforts to bring the canoes down river, allowing himself time to go to Massassa Falls in a canoe to visit the place where my dear Frank was lost. Rashness and imprudence! To venture before he had viewed the scene himself. Had he exercised but the slightest caution, he had been alive today to gladden me with his society. On June 19th all the canoes had passed the fearful Bolo-Bolo and arrived safely at Zinga.

June 20th:

Halt. Zinga Falls.

A STRANGE DAY! After reading the remarks written June 15th, 1877, I appear to have divined that some event was imminent. On calling the Wangwana together to muster, I addressed them a few words to the effect that unless we were able to clear ourselves from these Falls within a month, we shall be at the mercy of the natives from danger of starvation; that every man should do his duty now as if he were fighting for soul and body. I separated the best men from the inveterate idlers, and said to the latter: "You are those who bring us to this danger. You will not work, but you eat the rations of those who are willing to work", and to their Chief, Safeni, I said: "You have here 31 lazy fellows who wish to ruin us. They say they are tired. Hold a palaver with these men as to what is the best thing to do: to work with might and main to clear these Falls and so get away to somewhere where we can get food, or die amongst these savage people from starvation. When you have done your palaver, I shall return to hear the result of it; meanwhile I go to set work for those who, I know, are willing to assist me".

196

After I had gone, one of the idlers said to Safeni: "Well, Father, what is the best thing for us to do?" "Roll up your mats, and march away from here", said he. And the 31 men with one consent rolled up their mats and started up the slope of the mountain for the sea! When I returned they were all gone! I instantly despatched messengers after them to request them to pause and reflect upon the certain death they would incur from such blind conduct. They have no money. They could speak no language. They had no arms to defend themselves from any tribe who might be induced by their helplessness to enslave them. Safeni in a rage would not stop and his men followed him for 6 hours march when they halted for rest. I sent other messengers to warn them, to invite them to return. They refused and the messengers returned unsuccessful, though they told the [*local*] tribe not to let my people pass until they should hear again from me.

June 21*st:*

Halt. Zinga Falls.
Yesterday and today busy preparing the road across Zinga Point to haul the canoes.
Sent Manwa Sera and Kacheche again to the mutineers with express invitation and command to return. For 3 hours he laboured hard to persuade them to return, but they only consented to do so when Manwa Sera threatened to call the natives to bind them and bring them to camp as prisoners. Safeni was the first who proposed returning.

June 22*nd:*

Halt. Zinga Falls.
The mutineers returned last night, but I did not reprove them. In the afternoon, the great canoe *Livingstone* was being hauled up, when the cables broke and she darted down the hill to the river dragging one of my best men with her, Salaam Allah, the carpenter and builder of the canoe. Three men swam out to rescue him but the stream was swift and a few yards below were the Falls and Whirlpools of Zinga. Salaam Allah feared to trust himself to the men, so he and the canoe were swept over the Falls, tossed up and down by the huge waves, finally sucked in 3 times, and he was drowned. The canoe was

followed by land as far as Mbelo, whirled round five times and disappeared for ever.

June 23rd:

Halt. Zinga Falls.

Was 5 hours hauling the large canoe *Cheandoah* up a hill 200 feet high. Have only 7 canoes and boat now. Uttermost they will carry, 198 men. Hear of a place called Kakongo below all the Falls where they propose to fight us simply for the glory of it, it seems, for so far reports have all been in our favour. No one has been injured or insulted. We have been on the best of terms with all natives, but Kakongo on the left bank long before we appear, it seems, make ready for war.

On June 27th, which was the 25th day after Stanley's arrival at Zinga Falls, the Expedition set out again, covering a distance of 2 miles to Mbelo where there was another set of rapids to be passed. These did not prove so difficult, though a ram which Stanley had acquired at Asama in early January and was reserving for Baroness Burdett Coutts fell down a cliff 200 feet deep and broke both forefeet, also ribs. The ill-fated canoe in which Frank had been drowned was discovered broken in two pieces at the foot of the Falls but, although news was heard from time to time of Frank's body floating down the river, his remains were never recovered.

July 12th:

Lukalu. Descend river 2 miles.

Ferouz Baraka died of ulcerous sores on feet and legs, literally eaten up with them. While on the mountain plateau [*west of Mowa*] all the Wangwana were subject to a pestilent boring worm very like a wood borer, which bored deep into the toes and deposited eggs and formed ulcers.

July 13th:

Descended Mansau Falls and 2 Rapids and camped a few yards above Matunda Rapids opposite Upper Kakongo, that terrible fighting country against which we had many times been warned by people of Zinga, Mowa and Mbelo. Numbers of

Kakongo people came across shooting rapids. Kindly gentle amiable people, preferable to us than any except Nzabi and [*Gamfwa?*].

July 14*th:*

Descended Matunda Rapids to Ngoyo. Kakongo people visited us by scores from opposite side.

On July 15*th a great market was held and the next day* 409 *persons of both sexes assembled on a rocky point to watch the Expedition as it arrived at the Ngombi Falls.*

July 17*th:*

Halt.

200 stalwart natives offered themselves voluntarily to take our canoes across the Falls for three cloths, which was readily accepted. By noon we had passed the Falls, but one small canoe was ruined, leaving us only 6 and the boat, which was in a wretched condition.

On July 18*th Stanley made the following note:*
In briefly summing up today what we had effected worthy of note, I was somewhat abashed at the apparent boastfulness of the summary. Yet it is not half as striking as the details:

We have attacked and destroyed 28 large towns and three or four score villages, fought 32 battles on land and water, contended with 52 Falls and Rapids, constructed about 30 miles of tramway work through Forests, hauled our canoes and boat up a mountain 1,500 feet high, then over the mountains 6 miles, then lowered them down the slope to the river, lifted by rough mechanical skill our canoes up gigantic boulders 12, 15 and 20 feet high, then formed a tramway over these boulders to pass the falls of Massassa, Nzabi and Zinga. All this since leaving Nyangwe [*November 5th,* 1876].

We obtained as booty in wars over $50,000 worth of ivory, 133 tusks and pieces of ivory, but with the loss of 12 Canoes and the loss of 13 lives, we lost nearly the whole of the ivory; thefts were also frequent and no precaution could preserve it from loss. Frank was lame and I superintended the work at the Falls, the Camp, and [*of*] the unprincipled thieves of the Expedition.

After Frank's loss thieving increased until I threatened to shoot the next convicted of theft. Our monies, beads, cloth, etc. were wasted in the same manner. Accidents at the Falls were frequent. Canoes were swept from our hands, men in them to utter destruction. In such cases loss of money appeared a small matter.

Had I the least suspicion that such a terrible series of Falls were before us, I should never have risked so many lives and such amount of money, but the natives whether from ignorance or interest constantly cheered us with the reports that only one or two remained, after which we might lie in the canoes and glide dreamily down river without danger.

The Expedition continued down stream without incident until on July 21st it reached Kibonda.

July 22nd:

Halt [*Kibonda*].

Contrary to repeated examples of theft and its consequent punishment, the men yesterday were certainly attacked with a stealing mania. Three were caught by the natives, but one broke loose from his captors by brandishing a knife, and one cut his cords in the night, but Hamadi refused to take advantage of his companion's release, as the natives had taken his gun away and stored it in another village.

The confusion rising from this raid upon a hitherto quiet district was extreme. Till late in the night I was kept up negotiating for the thief's release. We were also somewhat depressed in mind by being told with much circumstantial detail of three Falls ahead, one of which from its description I took to be "Tuckey's Cataract". If we took the man by force, we must of course lose the gun, for the alarm would be such that it would be immediately hid. Then for the sake of the thief alone to lose 20 or 30 lives and property, and to have to fight our way while passing the Falls over land was a losing policy. My Chiefs unanimously said: "Let him perish a thief's death. He has richly deserved it."

They abandoned the wretch and continued their journey, always anxious at rumours of more cataracts ahead.

July 26th:

Descend Itunzima Falls by Rapids on left bank and camp at a point below Falls on right.

The last 3 days I have been grieved by the sudden lunacy of one of my best Chiefs or Captains, Wadi Safeni. There has been no cause except it is hereditary for it. He has always been one of my favourites for his cleverness and cheerfulness. Today he broke his bonds and after embracing me in a most pathetic manner, he left. I immediately sent two men to follow him and bring him back but he could not be found. He had only a parrot with him which he carried on a stick. Poor Safeni, how will he fare now! I cannot stay as my goods are terribly short. I must haste, haste away from this hateful region of death, terror and barbarism, to kinder lands lest death by starvation overtake us.

With food scarce, natives unco-operative and cataracts frequent, the Expedition hungrily made its way down-river until, on reaching yet another cataract on July 30th—that of Isangila—Stanley heard from the natives that Embomma (now Boma), the European Trading Station furthest up country from the Atlantic Ocean, was only another six days' journey away by water. This notwithstanding, people are so tired and weak that I fear we must give up the River and trudge over land, as we hear there are four Falls yet.

July 31st:

Halt [*Isangila Cataract*].

We had a visit from three Kings today, two of whom brought a goat each, a few peanuts and a demijohn of palm wine, for which they received 3 *doti* each. The people are perfectly hateful to think of, with not one redeeming trait, insolent liars, poor and beggars. Here people sold addled eggs as chickens and wished to sell them for 1 cloth each.

We have decided to abandon the River as it is not in our power to continue the warfare longer. Tuckey's map is infamous for its errors and has been the prime cause of our fighting so long against natives.

August 1st:

Leave river, boat and canoes and start over land, and reach at noon 7 miles Ndambi Mbongo.

August 2nd:

March 8 miles and camp in wilderness.

Tough work over mountains. Terribly hungry. I fear for my people. Beads are almost useless, brass wire not in demand, nothing but cloth of which we have so little that it is like the widow's cruse of oil. Stones troublesome.

August 3rd:

Arrive at Nsanda 10 miles, a miserable little village of about 50 souls, who possess very many palm trees.

We are so hungry, I expect to hear that some of my people drop from hunger. Stones troublesome.

August 4th:

Halt.

Send Kacheche, Robert, Uledi the Coxswain and Muini Pembe to Embomma with guides and letters to English and French traders, praying for relief in the shape of rice, grain, or cloth.

People out all over the country exploring for food: the baobab, calabashes and any edible roots. One peck of potatoes cost 4 yards of cloth; beads and shells or wine of not much value here, the cloth is so plentiful that it is almost worthless.

Palm wine is abundant but for hungry men something more substantial is needed.

August 5th:

March to Mbinda 12 miles, a district of 16 or 17 villages. On the highest range crossed, Aneroid showed 2,100 feet. People amiable but terribly extortionate, and so keen in trading that my people get more and more emaciated.

These people are given up to the delights of palm wine and marketing women slaves, raise peanuts and a few potatoes etc. They are so lazy, that the country is almost inexplorable from the difficulty of procuring provisions.

August 6th:

March to Banza Mbuko 4 miles. A market was close by and I heard that cowries were in demand and I instantly gave 40 to each man to procure food.

August 7*th:*

March to N'lamba N'lamba 5 miles.

Soon after camping, Kacheche came with supplies. 5 gallons of Rum. 4 sacks of rice, 2 sacks of potatoes. 1 bag of tobacco. 3 large loads of fish and 1 load of sundry small things for myself such as tea, sugar, bread, butter, fish, jam, fruit in tin, English shag and cigarette paper, and three bottles of India Pale-Ale. The men gave three hearty cheers and a [*tiger?*] at the sight. The skeletonized men began to revive, and this afternoon there is not a soul but is joyful. The long war against famine is over.

August 8*th:*

March to N'safu 5 miles.

The country is very bare except in the immediate vicinity of the villages and very fatiguing to travel over, being so hilly.

Sent Robert and Zambarao after another demijohn of Rum.

August 9*th:*

Arrive at Embomma 5 miles on the Congo River.

Greeted by Europeans. Motta Veiga. J. W. Harrison. Pinto. Henriques. Mr. Price. Captain of St[*eamer*] *Kabinda.*

August 10*th,* 1877.

Halt [*At Boma*].

It was the 1,000*th day since the Anglo-American Expedition had set out from Zanzibar. The Wangwana were shipped home round the Cape to Zanzibar, and Stanley sailed for England.*

SELECTIVE INDEX OF PERSONS

Denotes member of Expedition

A

Abdul Azziz Bey, *see* Linant de Belle-fonds, 107
Abed bin Salim, Arab merchant, 133
*Akida, 78
*Alassi Jumbe, 55
Antari, King of Ihangiro, 75, 76, 92, 96

B

Bakumu, tribe on the Congo, 150, 151, 155
*Barker, Frederick, xiii, 38, 47, 60, 72, 78, 81
Bateke, tribe on the Congo, 167, 171, 172, 181
Bennett, Sir John, 98
*Billali, xiii, 30
Broyon, Swiss trader, 119
*Bull, Stanley's bulldog, 39, 105, 107, 114
Burdett-Coutts, Baroness, 25, 198
Burton, Richard, explorer, x, 52, 78

C

Cameron, Lt. V. L., R.N., explorer, xi, xiii, xvii, 129, 132, 135
Captain, a mastiff dog, 27
Castor, a mastiff dog, 25
*Chakanja, 50
Chalula, King of Mukondoku, 38
*Chowpereh, xiii, 98

D

*Dallington, 108

E

Emin Pasha, Governor of Sudanese Equatoria, viii, ix, xiii

F

*Farjalla, xiii, 49
*Ferahan, xiii, 50
*Ferouz Baraka, 198
*Fundi Rehani, 87

G

*Gardner, 56
Grant, Colonel J. A., explorer, 71, 78, 107

H

*Hamadi, 200
Hamed bin Mohammed, *see* Tippu-Tib
Hamed Hamudi, *see* Tippu-Tib
Hamed Ibrahim, 117
Hancock, U.S. General, ix
*Hedi, 55

I

Itsi of Itamo

J

*Jabiri, 78
*Jack, Stanley's bull-terrier, 39, 98, 107
*Jumah Dipsingessi, 58, 59
Jumah Merikani, Arab trader, 132

K

Kabba Rega, King of Unyoro, 110
*Kacheche, xiii, 111, 112, 130, 139, 183, 186, 187, 189, 194, 197, 202, 203
Kaduma, Chief of Kagehyi, 63, 78, 81, 86
*Kaif Halleck, 47, 48
*Kalulu, xiii, 130, 133, 174, 177, 181
Kamoÿdah, Chief of Kefweh, 67, 68
Keelusu of Mwenna, Prince, 38
Khamis bin Abdullah, Arab trader, 72
Kijaju, King of Komeh, 87

L

Leopold II, King of the Belgians, ix
Linant de Bellefonds, Colonel, 71, 73, 74
Livingstone, David, explorer, viii, ix, x, xi, xv, 47, 56, 70, 73, 78, 111, 120, 122, 125, 129, 135, 159, 171
Long, Colonel, otherwise Long Bey, 71, 107
Lukongeh, Sultan of Ukerewe, 81, 82, 83

M

*Mabruki, xiii, 175, 176, 177
*Mabruki Manyapara, 133
*Mabruki Speke, 78
Magassa, Admiral of Uganda, xiv, 69, 74, 75, 88, 89, 98, 99
Magura, Chief Admiral of Uganda, 75
Mahdi, The, Sudanese patriot, viii
Mansur bin Suleiman, Governor of Bagamoyo, 25
*Manwa Sera, Captain General of the Expedition, xiii, 42, 51, 86, 91, 92, 140, 152, 162, 163, 184, 189, 193, 194, 197
Marewa, Chief of the Mgongo Tembo, 52, 53, 54

205

Indices

*Marzouk, 154
Masai, tribe in East Africa, 29, 30
Masumami, Chief of Kitalalo, 36, 38
*Membe, 87
Milton, John, poet, 102
Mirambo, Lord of the Ruga-Ruga, xiv, 40, 52, 56, 57, 58, 71, 81, 117, 118, 119
Miryamwezi, people of Mirambo, 118
*Mkamanga, 55
Mohammed bin Gharib, Arab trader, 120
Mohammed bin Sali, Arab trader, 120
*Mohammed the Somali, 36
*Msenna, 30, 78
Mtagamoyo, xiii, 134, 141, 160
Mtesa, King of Uganda, xiv, xv, xix, 39, 69, 70, 71, 72, 73, 75, 76, 81, 82, 88, 89, 91, 92, 97, 98, 99, 100, 101, 102, 103, 104, 105, 106, 107, 108, 110, 114, 118
Mtibula, see Tippu-Tib
*Muccadum, 98
*Muftah Rufigi, 157
Muini Dugumbi, henchman of Tippu-Tib, xiii, 134
Muini Hassan, 147
Muini Kheri, Arab trader, 120
Muini Kibwana, henchman of Tippu-Tib, 134
Muini Mubara, 14
*Muini Pembe, 202
Muley bin Salim, Islamic apostle of Uganda, 71
Murabo, 50
*Muscati, 146, 147, 152

N

*Nero, Stanley's Newfoundland dog, 32, 33

P

*Pocock, Edward, xiii, 32, 46, 47
*Pocock, Francis (Frank), xiii, xvi, xviii, 31, 32, 47, 60, 78, 81, 86, 98, 105, 109, 114, 129, 130, 138, 141, 142, 146, 168, 171, 179, 186, 187, 189, 190, 191, 192, 193, 194, 195, 198, 199, 200

R

*Rehani, 174, 177
*Robert, 119, 202, 203
*Rojab, 146
*Rowlands, John, otherwise Stanley, H. M., viii
Ruga-Ruga, tribe of brigands, xiv, 57, 81, 118, 119, 120
Rumanika, King of Karagwe, xiv, 114, 115, 116

S

*Saburi Jumbe, 55
*Saburi Rehani, 185
*Safeni, 50, 196, 197

*Salaam Allah, 197
Salim bin Sayf, Arab trader, 123
Sambuzi, General of Uganda, xiv, 107, 108, 109, 110, 111, 112, 113, 114
Savory & Moore, chemists, 115
Sayid bin Habib, Arab trader, 132
Sayid bin Mohammed, Arab trader, 119
Schweinfurth, German explorer, 135
Shekka, King of Bumbireh, 90, 96
*Soudi of Ituru, 175, 176, 177, 178
Speke, John Hanning, explorer, x, 52, 70, 71, 78, 107, 114
Stanley, American broker, ix
*Suleiman, 49

T

Tennant, Dorothy, x
Theodore, King of Abyssinia, ix
Tippu-Tib, Arab trader, xiii, 132, 134, 136, 137, 139, 143, 144, 145
Tuckey, Captain, R.N., explorer, xi, 201

U

*Uledi, xiii, 152, 153, 178, 154, 179, 189, 190, 202

W

*Wadi Ambari, 175, 176, 177
*Wadi Baraka, 190, 191
*Wadi Rehani, xiii, 189
*Wadi Safeni, xiii, 201
Waganda, the people of Uganda, xiv, 69, 70, 88, 91, 92, 93, 95, 97, 98, 100, 101, 102, 103, 104, 108, 110, 111, 112, 113, 114
Wagenya, 138, 140, 156
Wagogo, the people of Ugogo, 35, 37, 38, 40
Wakerewe, the people of Ukerewe, 82, 83, 95
*Wangwana, Stanley's people, xiii, 25, 38, 41, 75, 88, 93, 95, 104, 109, 110, 111, 112, 132, 141, 169, 184, 191, 194, 195, 196, 198, 203
Wanyamwezi, Tippu-Tib's people, xiii, 41, 55, 57, 117, 124, 144, 145
Wanyaturu, the people of Ituru, 50, 51, 53
Wanyoro, the people of Unyoro, 110, 114
Waregga, the people of Uregga, 138
Wasagara, the people of Usagara, 28, 110, 112
Wasukuma, the people of Usukuma, 41, 54, 55, 56, 59
Watuta, a band of nomadic roughs, 119
Wavuma, the people of Uvuma, xv, 98, 100, 101, 102, 103, 104

Z

*Zaidi, xiii, 152, 153, 154
*Zambarao, 179, 203
*Zazinie, a dog from Zanzibar, 107

Indices

INDEX OF NEWSPAPERS AND BOOKS

Daily Telegraph, ix, 63, 135, 195
Figaro, 119
How I found Livingstone, 31

New York Herald, ix, 63, 135, 195
Through the Dark Continent, ix, xii, xiii, xv,
xvi, xvii, xviii

INDEX OF VESSELS

Cheandoah, a canoe, 198
Lady Alice, a collapsible boat, xiii, 25, 52,
63, 64, 78, 153, 187, 189

Livingstone, a canoe, 197

SELECTIVE INDEX OF PLACES

B

Bagamoyo, 25, 53
Baswa Banki Rapids, 148, 149
Battle Cove, 76
Bolo-Bolo, Basin of, 189, 190, 194, 196
Boma, ix, xii, xix, 201, 202, 203
Brazzaville, 171
Burton Bay, 124

C

Chiwyu (*modern* Suna), xiii, 44, 45, 46
Chumbiri, 167, 168, 169
Congo Free State, vii, viii, ix, 171

D

Denbigh, N. Wales, viii
Dover Cliffs, 170, 171
Dumo, xiv, 97, 98, 105, 107

E

Embomma, *see* Boma

F

Furzehill Place, Pirbright, vii, x

G

Gambaragara Mt. (Mt. Gordon-Bennett),
113
Gamfwa's Bay, 179, 181, 199
Gavubu's Bay, 179
Gondoroko, xii, 135

I

Ihangiro, 89, 90, 91, 93, 95, 96
Ikondu, 142, 148
Ingulufi Falls, 189
Iramba, 52, 53, 54, 64
Isangila Falls, 201
Islands in Lake Victoria:
Alice, 91
Barker's, 75

Bridge, 66
Bumbireh, 75, 81, 86, 88, 89, 90, 91,
92, 93, 94, 95, 96, 97, 98, 99
Burdett-Coutts, 65
Dobo, 65
Ingira, 100
Iroba, 88, 89, 90, 91, 92, 93, 96
Ito, 85
Komeh, 83, 84, 87
Magu, 59, 64
Mahyiga, 88, 89, 90, 91, 92, 93, 98
Miandereh, 84, 85
Ngevi, 67, 68
Refuge, 77, 85, 87, 91, 92
Sesse, 74, 75, 98, 102
Sima, 59
Singo, 85
Uvuma, 69, 98, 100
Islands in the RR. Lualaba, Congo:
Asama, 155, 156, 198
Cheandoah, 150, 151
Juemba, 172
Kalulu, 176
Ntunduru, 151, 152, 155
Itunzima Falls, 201
Ituru, 47, 48, 49, 50, 51, 52

J

Jinja, 99, 105
Jiweh la Singa, 37, 53
Jiweni (Granite Boulders), 35
Jiweni (The Rocks), 43, 44

K

Kafurro, 114, 115, 116, 117
Kagehyi, xiii, xiv, xv, xviii, 59, 60, 63,
74, 75, 77, 78, 81, 83, 85, 86, 87
Kajurri, 89, 93
Karagwe, xiii, 70, 114, 115
Kazinga, 115
Kibonda, 200
Kima-Kima, 137, 145

207

Kirurumo, 37, 40
Kitalalo, 35, 36, 37, 38
Kitangeh, 29, 31

L

Lakes:
  Lake Albert or Muta Nzige (properly
    L. Edward) 97, 98, 99, 103, 107, 109,
    113
  Lake Tanganyika, viii, ix, x, xi, xiii,
    xvii, xix, 114, 116, 120, 121, 129
  Lake Victoria, viii, x, xi, xiv, xv, xix,
    37, 52, 53, 59, 60, 63, 64, 78, 87, 116,
    119
  Lake Windermere, 114
Lambeth, N., x
Leopoldville, 171

M

Mansau Falls, 198
Manyema, xiv, 131, 132, 171
Massassa Falls, 187, 189, 190, 194, 195,
  196, 199
Massesse Falls, 187, 190
Matunda Rapids, 198, 199
Mgongo Tembo, 48, 51, 52, 53, 54, 55
Mombiti, 54, 55, 56, 57
Mowa, vii, 186, 187, 188, 192, 193, 194,
  198
Mpwapwa, 28, 29, 30, 31
Mtowa or Arab Crossing-place, 129, 130
Mukondoku, 36, 37, 38, 39, 40
Murchison Bay, 69

N

Nakaranga, 100, 102, 104, 105
Napoleon Channel, 69
New Orleans, U.S.A., ix
Ngombi Falls, 199
Nseto Falls, 186
Nyangwe, x, xi, xii, xiii, xvii, 129, 132,
  133, 134, 136, 144, 146, 171, 199
Nzabi, 185, 186, 199

R

Ripon Falls, x, 69, 98, 99
Rivers
  Aruwimi (Battle river), 158, 159
  Coango, 136, 137
  Congo, vii, viii, ix, xi, xii, xiii, xv,
    xvi, xix, 25, 116, 129, 137, 171,
    172, 173, 174, 181, 182, 183, 187,
    189, 203
  Juemba, 171, 172
  Kagera, 97, 114, 115
  Katonga, 74, 97, 102, 108, 113
  Livingstone, xiii, xv
  Lualaba (Lualawa, Ugarowa), x, xi,
    xii, xv, 132, 133, 135, 136, 137, 138,
    139, 141, 142, 143, 159
  Luama, 131, 132
  Lukuga, 123
  Malagarazi, 116

Mukondokwa (Wami), 27, 28, 29
Nile, viii, ix, x, 25, 116, 135
Rufiji, 37, 39
Ruiki, 139, 140
Rumami, 137, 145
Victoria Nile, 69
White Nile, xii
Ruanda, 114, 115, 130
Rubaga, 105, 106
Rubunga, 160, 161, 162

S

St. Asaph Union Workhouse, ix
Speke Gulf, 59, 64, 81, 83
Stanley Pool, 171
Stanleyville, 156
Suna, *see* Chiwyu
Sundi Cataract, 165

T

Tuckey's Farthest, xi, 200

U

Uganda, xiii, xv, 70, 74, 81, 82, 83, 85,
  86, 87, 89, 91, 92, 97, 99, 104, 106,
  108, 109, 111, 112, 113, 114, 135,
  138
Ugogo, 29, 31, 32, 33, 35, 36, 37, 40, 41
Ujiji, ix, xi, 120, 121, 123, 126, 129, 130,
  131, 134, 177
Ukerewe, 59, 63, 64, 81, 82, 83, 91, 98
Ulagalla, 73, 74, 105
Unyanyembe (*modern* Tabora), 38, 40,
  52, 78
Unyoro, 70, 109, 110, 114
Uregga, xvii, xviii, 134, 136, 138
Urimi, 41, 43, 44, 45
Urundi, 115
Ururi, 63, 64, 65
Usagara, 25, 26, 28, 29
Usavara, 69, 70, 71, 72, 73, 74, 103
Usiha, 56, 57, 58
Usukuma, 55, 56, 57, 58, 59, 74, 75, 82,
  85, 86
Uveriveri (Were-Were), 42, 43

V

Vinya-Njara, xiii, 144
Vinyata, 47, 48, 49, 50

W

Wenya Falls, 156, 147

Y

Yellala Cataract, 182, 165

Z

Zanzibar, ix, xii, xiii, xiv, xix, 25, 30,
  31, 41, 52, 58, 71, 74, 96, 108, 117,
  135, 137, 193, 203
Zinga, 187, 189, 192, 193, 194, 195,
  196, 197, 198, 199